TELLY ADDICT
SOAPS

TELLY ADDICT
SOAPS

First published in the UK in 2014

© Demand Media Limited 2014

www.demand-media.co.uk

Printed and bound in Europe

ISBN 978-1-910270-05-9

Contents

Introduction

The term 'soap opera' originated from America in the 1930s. Popular television and radio series were sponsored by major manufacturers of cleaning and household products. Goods such as soap powder were advertised during a programme's commercial break in the hope of increasing network ratings and profits. The word 'opera' became part of the term due to the reference of a story developing, evolving and unfolding in a melodramatic style. Today, the term 'soaps' has been adopted as a more popular phrase.

Telly Addict: Soaps highlights over thirty well-known and loved soap operas that have given pleasure to British audiences for many years, in fact some of them for decades. The variety and diversity of soap operas produced over the past seventy or so years is quite staggering. From the 1950s BBC radio's world's longest-running radio soap The Archers, The Grove Family on television to Emergency Ward 10, Coronation Street and EastEnders, many have become household favourites that are still watched avidly by fans with many being repeated regularly on the many television networks now available with digital channels.

In addition to the numerous soap operas themselves, many of the actors and actresses – some who launched their careers by starring in them – have also become renowned and distinguished figures. Personalities such as Barbara Windsor and Kylie Minogue are just some of the famous and acclaimed actors and actresses who have starred in the soap operas showcased here.

TELLY ADDICT : **SOAPS**   5

A Country Practice

A Country Practice was a very popular, award-winning, Australian series that began on the 18th November 1981 and ran for 12 years. The series was initially broadcast on Australia's Seven Network for 1,058 episodes. Producer James Davern became known to the network when he entered a scriptwriting competition and won 3rd place; his entry was used for the pilot episode.

Viewers were fascinated by the residents of the fictional town set in Wandin Valley and storylines centred on the small medical practice in New South Wales. In 1994, the Ten Network commissioned a further 30 episodes, and with many new cast members, the show ran for another 7 months.

Iconic storylines include the wedding of Dr. Simon Bowen, (Grant Dodwell) to local vet Vicki Dean (Penny Cook) in 1983, and the later wedding of Dr. Terence Elliot (Shane Porteous) to Matron Rosemary Prior. Also, the death of Nurse Donna Manning (Caroline Johansson) in a car crash and the off-screen death of resident Shirley Gilroy in a plane crash (Lorrae Desmond). The highest rating episode featured the death of Molly Jones (Anne Tenney) from Leukaemia.

A Country Practice enjoyed a worldwide weekly audience of up to 6 million at its peak. The show became very well known for cameo roles and the appearances of guest stars, including Baz Luhrmann, Smokey Dawson, John Meillon, Sir Robert Helpmann, Australian Prime Minister Bob Hawke, Nicole Kidman, Toni Collette, Delta Goodrem, Peter Phelps and Simon Baker The success of the series was partly

attributed to the international appeal of the native Australian animals and wildlife featured in every episode. Fatso the wombat was a particular favourite. The series was also renowned for examining topical issues and raising awareness of current affairs. The storylines examined youth unemployment, suicide, drug addiction, HIV/AIDS, chronic conditions and the history of Aborigines and their transition into Australian society. A Country Practice won 'Best Series' many times and an admirable 29 Logie Awards in total.

Angels

St Angela's hospital in Battersea was the focus of this popular British medical series. The first episode was aired on BBC1 on 1st September 1975 and followed the lives of student nurses at the south London hospital. Although the title of the show came from the hospital called St Angela's, based in Wandsworth, during the 1980s the setting changed to Heath Green Hospital in Birmingham.

The highly successful drama was created by Paula Milne and ran for 220 episodes; the last was broadcast in December 1983. Every member of the cast had to undergo work experience at a hospital to make their performance credible and accurate. Writers were also expected to carry out their research at real hospitals. Writers on the first series included Jill Hyem and Anne Valery who both went on to write the popular dramatised series Tenko. The first episode of Angels was directed by Julia Smith who became the show's producer in 1979. Her script editor on the later series was Tony Holland. Julia Smith and Tony Holland both enjoyed further success on Eastenders in the 1980s.

The controversial drama was a springboard for the development of a number of actresses who later enjoyed fame and popularity. Angels starred Lesley Dunlop, Pauline Quirke, Lynda Bellingham, Fiona Fullerton and Angela Bruce. Other members of the cast went on to join EastEnders.

Angels received a great deal of criticism at times because of the way student nurses were depicted. Characters were wrapped in storylines involving alcoholism and promiscuity. Sensitive topics relating to

the demands facing young nurses in their profession were portrayed but widely criticised. Angels is believed to have been the original blueprint for medical soaps such as Casualty, Holby City and Doctors.

Beverley Hills, 90210

An American soap opera commencing on the 4th October 1990 that became hugely popular with teenagers. The programme was named after one of the three regional postal codes (zip codes) in Beverley Hills California. Twins Brandon (Jason Priestly) and Brenda Walsh (Shannen Doherty) are the focus of the early episodes as they experience a new life in Beverley Hills, which is in stark contrast to their previous home in Minneapolis. In addition to this it follows the lives of their peer group, highlighting friendship issues, romance and related family backgrounds.

The show also tackled serious topical issues such as date rape, gay rights, animal rights, alcoholism, domestic violence, anti-Semitism, drug abuse, teenage suicide, teenage pregnancy, AIDS, bulimia and abortion. Beverly Hills, 90210 was subsequently named one of the Best School Shows of All Time by AOL TV.

Torrance High School, located in zip code 90501, was used as the set for the fictional West Beverly High School. The same location was used to film scenes in Buffy the Vampire Slayer. During the 10 years the series was in production, it was filmed in a warehouse complex in Van Nuys.

The series was created by Aaron Spelling, Darren Star and E. Duke Vincent, first broadcast by Fox and ran for 10 seasons and a total of 293 episodes. After enjoying enormous popularity, the final episode aired on the 17th May 2000. The entire original cast, excluding Shannen Doherty and Douglas Emerson, appeared in the series finale.

Production companies included Torand Productions, Propaganda

Films and Spelling Television. Torand Productions was used by the production company for several seasons of the show. The name Torand productions was derived from the first three letters of Aaron Spelling's first child, Tori and the first four letters of his second child, Randy. Actresses Tori Spelling, Shannen Doherty and Jennie Garth became household names in America. Ratings increased, particularly when Jason Priestley and Luke Perry became teen idols. The show had many cast changes but Jennie Garth, Tori Spelling, Ian Ziering and Brian Austin Green were regulars throughout.

Ten awards were won during the 10-year history of the soap opera and included BMI Film & TV Awards, Young Artist Awards and Tp de Oro twice awarded Beverley Hills 90210 'Best Foreign Series'.

Brookside

A classic ground-breaking British soap and often referred to as 'the ultimate soap'. Brookside was created by Phil Redmond (who also devised Grange Hill and Hollyoaks). Brookside began in 1982, set in Liverpool, Merseyside. 4.2 million viewers watched the first episode that coincided with the launch day of Channel 4. After 21 years, the soap went off air on the 4th November 2003, watched by just over 2 million viewers. Brookside brought together working and middle-class families in a contemporary environment.

Brookside was produced by Mersey Television and was originally going to be called Meadowcroft. Brookside had a unique setting due to Phil Redmond purchasing an entire 'close' of 13 houses. He believed this would add to the authenticity and realism of the show.

Brookside featured 6 households and 16 characters at the start. Starring Sheila Grant (Sue Johnston) and Bobby Grant (Ricky Tomlinson). The Grants were the first family to have moved onto the close and occupied number 5. The Collins family moved into number 8. Heather (Amanda Burton) and Roger Huntington (Rob Spendlove) lived at number 9 and they took an immediate dislike to the Grants. Newly-weds Gavin (Daniel Webb) and Petra Taylor (Alexandra Pigg) moved into number 10. Pensioners Harry (Bill Dean) and Edna Cross (Betty Alberge) bought number 7. The infamous Corkhills arrived in 1985.

Brookside is famed for soap opera 'firsts' and controversial storylines. The first pre-watershed lesbian kiss between Beth Jordache (Anna Friel) and Margaret Clemence (Nicola Stephenson) prompted

a flurry of complaints. A storyline involving an incestuous relationship between two siblings caused uproar. Brookside was the first soap to feature the emergence of an openly gay character, Gordon Collins (Nigel Cowley). Serious drug addiction was also portrayed for the first time and involved several characters. Media interest was at a peak as the story of domestic abuse victim Mandy Jordache (Sandra Maitland) reached a crescendo as she murdered her husband Trevor Jordache (Bryan Murray) and hid his body under the patio. That particular storyline was inspired by a real life case in Wallsall, West Midlands: an abused wife killed her husband and hid his body under the garden patio where he lay undiscovered for two years. The Brookside version resulted in the acquittal of Mandy Jordache who went on to have a baby with popular character Sinbad (Michael Starke). Brookside's longest-running character Jimmy Corkhill was played by Dean Sullivan and another favourite character was Barry Grant (Paul Usher).

Many early storylines were issue-led and strongly focused around Bobby and Sheila's turbulent marriage, which made compelling viewing. In 1986 Sheila Grant was at the centre of a hard hitting storyline, a controversial violent rape. The second big storyline of 1986 was intentionally shocking as Brookside heralded another 'first' and tackled heroin addiction in depth. Plots were extremely diverse and varied in popularity; some critics derided the more implausible plots. Religious cult Leader Simon Howe (Lee Hartney) brainwashed Terry Sullivan and Katie Rogers, taking over and then blowing up number 5 in a suicide pact during 1994. Another dubious narrative focused on a mysterious 'killer virus'. The close was quarantined and resulted in the death of three characters. During the show's 21 years, there were six catastrophic fires and explosions, including a faulty gas cooker that destroyed Brookside Parade. Claire Sweeney's character was affectionately referred to in the press as Lindsey 'Get Your Gun' Corkhill as the character became associated with so many plots involving guns. A hostage siege on the close culminated in a spectacular stunt as a police helicopter was shot down. The abandoned Brookside set was later used as a production set for Hollyoaks, Grange Hill and for the last time by horror film 'Salvage'.

Casualty

The world's longest running medical television series, created by Jeremy Brock and Paul Unwin. Casualty was first brought to our screens on September 6th 1986. The title sequence featured a speeding pink ambulance arriving at Holby City Emergency department with a police escort. The hospital is located in fictional Wyvern County, south west England. Production filming was originally based in Bristol but has now relocated to Cardiff. Holby City General has remained a frantically busy emergency department throughout the 28 series and more than 900 episodes. The programme charts the personal and professional lives of staff and patients. Storylines are often criticised for the graphic and controversial content, encompassing a diverse range of clinical and ethical issues. Award-winning make-up produces realistic, gory wounds and injuries that contribute to the success of Casualty and which has been recognised by The British Academy Television Awards.

The original cast focused on 10 characters. Amongst the most popular was senior house officer Baz Samuels (Julia Watson), consultant Ewart Plimmer (Bernard Gallagher), nurse Megan Roach (Brenda Fricker), student nurse Lisa 'Duffy' Duffin (Cathy Shipton) and charge nurse Charlie Fairhead (Derek Thompson) – the only remaining original character. New personalities form a growing cast list of multicultural and multiracial characters working for the NHS. It has been established that Casualty has featured more future stars than any other UK soap or drama series. Actors who appeared in the show prior to becoming famous include Kate Winslet, Orlando

Bloom, Minnie Driver, Christopher Eccleston, Tom Hiddleston, Parminder Nagra, Sadie Frost, Ray Winstone, David Walliams, Jonny Lee Miller, Martin Freeman, Helen Baxendale, Robson Green and Brenda Fricker.

Casualty often reflects current issues and medical trends. The Royal College of Nursing has noticed an increase in people who start a medical career later in life. Casualty has acknowledged this in the portrayal of character Fletch, a car mechanic with a failed business who retrained as a nurse. Popular characters Josh (Ian Bleasedale), Jeff (Matt Bardock) and Dixie (Jane Hazelgrove) play paramedics and are accredited with inspiring individuals to train in the profession.

Casualty has generated two spin-off series. Holby City chronicles the lives of doctors, nurses, ancillary staff and patients in connection with the surgical wards and operating theatres at Holby City Hospital. Holby Blue focused on the police services of Holby South but poor ratings resulted in it being axed after two series. There have been a number of occasions where staff from Casualty crossover with Holby City. Most recently nurse Fletch (Alex Walkinshaw) left the frenetic emergency department and became a permanent member of staff on the wards of Holby City General.

Iconic and memorable storylines include the affair of Charlie and Baz, a toxic gas outbreak, Duffy's rape, Megan's cancer battle, a siege, explosions and fire blazing through the department. Casualty has won 7 awards, achieving a BAFTA in 2007 for best continuing drama.

Coronation Street

One of the nation's best-loved soap operas. Tony Warren created the fictional street for Granada television in 1960 and initially wrote 13 pilot episodes. After three shows, the critics attacked and declared it would not last three weeks. Coronation Street is set in the fictional town of Weatherfield, Salford. The imaginary historical archives reveal that the street was built in 1900 and named in honour of the coronation of King Edward VII. The long-running soap originally focused on representing a down-to-earth, working-class community and chronicles the lives of residents and locals. The first episode to be transmitted in colour was in November 1969. The well-known theme music was written by Eric Spear, utilising instruments reminiscent of northern band music.

The show has both troughed and peaked in the ratings war over the years and has been redirected many times in order to reflect modern society and keep up-to-date with issue-driven storylines. Crossroads was a serious ratings rival at times, especially during the early 1970s. Original characters Ken Barlow (William Roache), Annie Walker (Doris Speed), Ena Sharples (Violet Carson), Minnie Caldwell (Margot Bryant) and Elsie Tanner (Pat Phoenix) all contributed to the show's public appeal. However, during a ratings decline, new regular characters were introduced in a bid to revive the number of viewers tuning in. Bet Lynch (Julie Goodyear), Ivy Tilsley (Lynne Perrie), Deidre (Ann Kirkbride) and Rita (Barbara Knox) joined the stalwart cast. Critics constantly condemned Coronation Street for being too serious

and focusing on the grim monotony of family affairs. A more comical, slapstick element was written into the script to lighten the mood and newcomers Vera and Jack Duckworth entered the show, joining Hilda and Stan Ogden, Eddie Yeats and Reg Holdsworth.

The programme currently rates as one of the most watched programmes on UK television. Viewership peaked in 1987 when 28.5 million viewers tuned in to see Hilda Ogden leave. With the arrival of EastEnders in 1985, the two programmes have been in a constant battle to secure first place in the ratings war. Coronation Street is the second most award-winning British soap opera in the UK; rival soap EastEnders is first.

Coronation Street has covered numerous storylines that received wide press attention, generating debate in the media and sometimes causing public outcry. Emily's husband Ernest was killed off in a bungled robbery at Mike Baldwin's factory and Granada's switchboard was jammed by angry viewers. Letters of complaint arrived in their hundreds. Brian Tilsley was fatally stabbed outside a nightclub. The stabbing brought a substantial amount of complaints from viewers and provoked Mary Whitehouse to deliver an angry speech about television violence. The wrongful imprisonment of Deirdre Rachid in 1998 prompted a media frenzy and the inception of the 'Free the Weatherfield One' campaign. Controversy often emanated from Anne Kirkbride and her character. Deirdre was attacked and subject to an attempted rape. Although the subject matter was very contentious, the storyline was responsible for encouraging women, who had been in the same situation, to confide in someone and seek help. An affair between Deidre and Mike Baldwin led to a bitter and continued feud between Ken and Mike. Throughout the decades, Coronation Street has witnessed fires, a coach crash, tram crashes, murder, a serial killer, rape, infant death, drug and alcohol addiction, prostitution, kidnap, euthanasia, a bisexual love triangle and plenty more! The intensity of traumatic plots has increased as the years progress. Ken Barlow's wife Valerie accidentally electrocuted herself due to faulty electrics and a hairdryer, a shocking incident in 1971.

In 1998, the Street introduced the first transsexual person in British soap history; Julie Hesmondhalgh married Roy Cropper. Although another controversial plot premise, this proved immensely popular and gained approval from transgendered groups. Coronation Street's first gay resident did not make an appearance until 2003 and critics felt Coronation Street was too slow to update their plots and reflect modern society. It was not until 1991 that Coronation Street introduced viewers to the first Asian family, Ravi, Nita and Vikram Desai. Upon occasion, Coronation Street script writers were almost instant in producing a current storyline. The disappearance of baby Freddie Peacock reflected the disappearance of Madeleine McCann in Portugal, which was ongoing simultaneously. As a result of this, the storyline was adjusted to ensure the McCann family were not offended.

On December 8th 2000, a special live episode of Coronation Street was broadcast to celebrate the programme's 40th anniversary. This was the first live episode since 1961, with guest appearances by Prince Charles, Noddy Holder and Sir Trevor McDonald. This format was so popular that it was revisited for the 50th anniversary and another live

show was broadcast on December 9th 2010, incorporating the misery of the second viaduct collapse in the show's history.

The street is famous for the 'Corrie Landmarks': The Rovers, The Kabin, Audrey's salon, the factory, The Red Rec, and surrounding cobbled streets, Rosamund Street, Inkerman Street, Bessie Street and Victoria Street. Originally filmed on set in Manchester, a new Coronation Street has been faithfully recreated in Trafford. An exact replica required 11,000 cobbles, 19,000 bricks and seven colours of mortar. Mawdsley Street is a recent addition that makes way for new characters to move into the famous street.

Crossroads

The UK's first, full length, daily soap. Episode one was screened on the 2nd November 1964, the series ran until 1988 the first time and from 2001 until 2003 on its second outing. Midland Road had been proposed as primary choice for the title but this was rejected in favour of Crossroads and featured Crossroads Motel and a shop, in fictional Kings Oak, near Birmingham. The title was changed again to Crossroads King's Oak. Tony Hatch composed the famous theme melody, later covered by Paul McCartney & Wings on their 1975 album Venus and Mars. A new theme tune accompanied the revamped series, composed by Raf Ravenscroft and Max Early.

Crossroads received mixed reviews and was often ridiculed for the wobbly set that affected the reputation of the soap opera for the entire run. The factory style production pace and fast turnaround schedule were considered responsible for weak scripts. However, the series gained many fans, most famously Prime Minister Harold Wilson's wife Mary. Crossroads often ran in second place to Coronation Street in the ratings league and occasionally gained first place. Created by Hazel Adair and Peter Ling, the format of the show was linked to their study of American Broadcasting and the desire to create a soap that was broadcast every day.

Noele Gordon starred in the leading role as character Meg Richardson until she was 'released from her contract' in 1981. Crossroads revolved around the lives of residents in the middle-class village, the Motel staff, guests and shop antics but the main focus was on the Richardson family.

The original foundation of Crossroads was based around two bickering sisters Kitty Jarvis (Beryl Johnstone) and Meg Richardson who married Charles, with whom she had two children, Jill and Alexander (known as Sandy). However, the most memorable character proved to be the sweet natured, simple-minded Benny Hawkins and his trademark woolly hat, worn throughout the year.

The series dealt with storylines deemed controversial at the time. A single parent working full time, paraplegic Sandy Richardson (Roger Tonge) used a wheelchair and was the first paraplegic regular character in a British soap opera. Melanie Harper (Cleo Sylvestre) arrived in 1970 as Meg's foster daughter, which was then a taboo topic. 1977 saw the introduction of a mixed–race relationship between Dennis Harper and motel receptionist

Meena Chaudri (Karan David). A rape, a test tube birth and the subject of Down's syndrome hit the headlines. Viewers saw an insight into the life of Nina Weill, soap opera's first Down's actress who portrayed Nina Paget. The plot covered bigoted views and unfavourable remarks made towards Nina by ignorant villagers. The story was praised by the press, the parents of Down's children and MENCAP.

After 12 years off air, Crossroads was revived in March 2001. Four characters from the original series returned: Doris Luke (Kathy Staff), Jill Harvey (née Richardson), Jill's ex-husband Adam Chance (Tony Adams), and Jill's daughter Sarah-Jane Harvey (Joanne Farrell/ Holly Newman). Jane Asher played a new character Angel Samson. Guest appearances featured, Kate O'Mara Lionel Blair, Les Dennis and Tim Brooke-Taylor.

The final episode was broadcast on Friday 30th May 2003. The poor close was slammed by critics and dubbed the 'The Dallas of Dudley'. The 75-minute episode featured Angel who realised her job as Hotel Manager had all been a dream and she returned to her 'real-life' job as a supermarket checkout assistant.

Dallas

An immensely popular American, prime-time television soap opera, that went to air on 2nd April 1978. The super soap was screened for 14 seasons. The series creator was David Jacobs and the theme music was composed by Jerrold Immel.

The show was notorious for its glossy portrayal of familial arguments, prosperity, scandal, intrigue and power struggles. Viewers eagerly awaited every episode, opening with sweeping panoramas of oil fields, cattle and skyscrapers. A recurring theme was the ever present and historic rivalry between the Ewing's of Texas and The Barnes family, heightened when Pamela Barnes (Victoria Principal) married Bobby Ewing (Patrick Duffy). This was a deeply despised union in the opinion of Pam's brother Cliff Barnes (Ken Kercheval).

The wealthy Ewings were immersed in riches derived from the ownership of their company Ewing Oil and the cattle farm enterprise at their homestead, Southfork Ranch. The eldest Ewing heir, oil tycoon J.R. (Larry Hagman) was infamous for his unscrupulous business dealings and he was also the only character to have appeared in every episode. J.R. was forever discontent in his marriage to long-suffering, alcohol dependant Sue Ellen (Linda Gray) who shot her husband twice and gained revenge in a blackmail reprisal. Parents Jock Ewing (Jim Davis) and Miss Ellie (Barbara Bel Geddes) were at the head of the family and were constant mediators of the feuding brothers. Middle son Gary (Ted Shackelford) married Valene (Joan Van Ark) and left the ranch and their daughter Lucy (Charlene Tilton). Additional characters saw the

development of musical actor Howard Keel as affluent rancher Clayton Farlow who married Miss Ellie after Jock's fatal aircraft accident. Priscilla Presley represented Bobby's teenage sweetheart Jenna Wade and Sue Ellen's scheming sister Kristin Shepard was played by Mary Crosby.

Dallas was renowned for its cliffhangers, the 'who shot J. R.?' story was a media triumph. The reveal episode unveiled perpetrator Kristen and the recorded viewership achieved an American audience of 90 million, a figure only surpassed by the last episode of M★A★S★H in 1983. The most poorly received storyline was Pam's dream as an explanation for Bobby's reappearance after his death in season eight. An equally dubious plot transpired when a replacement actress became the new Pamela, her physical differences explained away by the character needing emergency plastic surgery after a car accident in series ten. Patrick Duffy was asked to return in a bid to revive ratings, but the lustre of Dallas had become tarnished and the Southfork Ranch closed on 3rd May 1991. In the end, Cliff Barnes owned Ewing Oil, Bobby was the sole owner of Southfork and J.R. had nothing, not even an invitation to the Oil Baron's Ball. Dallas was revisited in a new series in 2012, featuring John Ross and Christopher Ewing. Both son's characters were the 'mini-me' of their fathers and the plots were a reincarnation of the aged family feuds.

Doctors

Doctors was a British television soap opera, first broadcast on the 27th March 2000, which was set in the fictional town of Letherbridge in the Midlands. It was created by Chris Murray. Filming originally took place at the BBC's Pebble Mill studios in Edgbaston, Birmingham and is now in production at a new BBC Drama Village development in Selly Oak, Birmingham.

The soap follows the staff and their families at the doctor's surgery, The Mill Health Centre, named after the series' original production home. Other regular locations include the police station, The Icon Bar and since 2008, The Campus Surgery. An episode typically sees the doctors and nurses of the practice meeting their patients at home or at the surgery and dealing with their ailments.

At one time, Doctors took lengthy breaks in transmission over the summer; it is currently an ongoing series but does take a break during the Wimbledon Tennis fortnight, at Christmas and at Easter.

Admired characters have included Christopher Timothy (Mac McGuire) and longest serving character Julia Parsons, played by Diane Keen. Also, Kate McGuire (Maggie Cronin) as Office Manager and a team of young doctors including Dr. Steve Rawlings (Mark Frost), Dr. Helen Thompson (Corrine Wicks), Dr. Rana Mistry (Akbar Kurtha) and Dr. Caroline Powers (Jacqueline Leonard). New characters were introduced in 2013: Dr. Emma Reid, her husband Sam and their son Chris.

Memorable storylines have involved a number of ill-fated receptionists: Donna Parmar broke patient confidentiality, which resulted in her sacking. Vivien

March's rape in 2008 caused a stir in the media and received recognition at The British Soap Awards in 2009. Karen Hollins fell pregnant and had an abortion and temporary receptionist Lauren Porter was murdered.

There have been a number of guest star appearances by Josie Lawrence, Ruth Madoc, Shaun Williamson, Lionel Blair and Louis Emmerick, who was a Brookside favourite. Two other former Brookside actors have also joined the show; Philip Oliver played 'Tinhead' and played a shockingly irrational gym manager in Doctors. Michael Starke, previously 'Sinbad 'in Brookside, portrayed a former security guard who was seeking revenge in Letherbridge.

The show has been nominated and won a variety of different awards. As of March 2014, Doctors has been nominated for 128 awards of which it has won 16.

Dynasty

A larger than life soap opera set in Denver Colorado. The extravagant show began on January 12th 1981, with the final episode being aired on 11th May 1989. The popular show portrayed the lives of the wealthy, glamorous and greedy. The production was predominantly filmed at the Filoli Estate in Woodside, California, utilising the 48-bedroom mansion. Dynasty was created by Richard and Esther Shapiro and produced by Aaron Spelling. The theme music was composed by Bill Conti.

Initially the show was dismissed as a poor relation of Dallas, featuring another rich family who made their fortune from oil. However, during the mid eighties, Dynasty was listed above Dallas in the ratings league.

The nation was fascinated with rich people and their diverse catalogue of troubles. During the height of the show's popularity, Former President Gerald Ford guest-starred as himself in 1983, with his wife Betty and Secretary of State Henry Kissinger. Hundreds of fans continuously wrote in to ask how they could obtain the extravagant dresses worn by Alexis and Krystle. The series costume designer Nolan Miller was asked to produce a range of haute couture garments called 'The Dynasty Collection'. The popularity of the show generated an enormous range of merchandising and even the development of signature perfume, cologne and linen collections.

The opulent soap opera began with oil tycoon, Blake Carrington (John Forsythe), falling in love with and

marrying his stunning, sweet natured secretary Krystle (Linda Evans). Blake's daughter Fallon (Pamela Sue Martin) strongly opposed the marriage. Fallon was one of a trio of characters that caused never-ending problems for Blake and Krystle. The other two were Blake's scheming ex-wife, Alexis (Joan Collins) and Krystle's ex Matthew Blaisdel (Bo Hopkins).

The second season began with Blake Carrington's trial; his sensational world was in utter turmoil. Blake had trouble accepting his son Steven (Al Corley) was a homosexual and accidentally killed Steven's ex-lover when he discovered them in an embrace. A surprise star witness testified against Blake and his ex-wife Alexis made a dramatic entrance to the series. After the trial, Alexis remained in Denver to wreak more havoc. Alexis intentionally fired a shot to startle Krystle's horse, resulting in Krystle's miscarriage and the battle between the two key females persisted as a continued theme.

As the seasons progressed, new characters were woven into the complicated family tree. Krystle's greedy niece Sammy Jo Dean (Heather Locklear) married Steven for his money. It was not uncommon for relatives to emerge from peculiar origins; Adam Carrington (Gordon Thomson) appeared as the long-lost son of Alexis and Blake who had been kidnapped in infancy. Alexis' secret daughter Amanda Bedford (Catherine Oxenberg) came to Denver and discovered that Blake is her father. Blake's illegitimate African American half-sister, Dominique Deveraux (Diahann Carroll), appeared in the latter seasons. The rivalry between Alexis and Krystle was a primary driver for the melodrama; their cat fights were both ridiculed and adored by fans. The fights also extended to other female characters: Dominique Deveraux fought her own cousin Sable Colby (Stephanie Beacham). Sammy Jo had catfights with Amanda (Catherine Oxenberg), Fallon (Emma Samms) and a slapping match with Claudia (Pamela Bellwood). Krystle even battled with herself at the climax of a 1985 to 1986 storyline in which Krystle is imprisoned and replaced by lookalike Rita, also played by Linda Evans.

The series evolved with numerous tragedies befalling the Carringtons and arson, kidnap and murder interspersed the glitz and glamour. Cliffhangers were expected at a season finale; undoubtedly the most famous was the 'Moldavian Massacre' during the 1985 season finale. Amanda and Prince Michael's royal wedding was interrupted by terrorists during a military coup in Moldavia. Bullets sprayed the church and it appeared that all of the major characters had been killed.

The cast saw frequent changes and key characters were replaced. Notable cast members included Rock Hudson, Kate O'Mara, Stephanie Beacham, Pamela Sue Martin, Lloyd Bochner, Michael Nader and Ted McGinley.

After nine seasons and 218 episodes, the show was cancelled. John Forsythe was the only cast member to appear in every episode. Dynasty 'The Reunion' was screened in 1991 to wrap up the loose ends of the series. The Colbys was a series spin-off but it did not flourish. Dynasty 11 was another short-lived spin-off that failed to thrive.

Dynasty won a Golden Globe Award for Best TV Drama Series in 1984. Linda Evans won Best Actress in 1982 and Joan Collins won in 1983.

EastEnders

One of the UK's highest-rated programmes that started on the 19th February 1985, EastEnders attracts an average eight million viewers per episode. Located in the imaginary London Borough of Walford, London E20 6PQ, fans have tried to establish the actual location of Walford within London. Walford East is a fictional tube station for Walford and with the aid of a map that was first seen on air in 1996, it has been established that Walford East is located between Bow Road and West Ham, which realistically would replace Bromley-by-Bow on the District and Hammersmith & City lines. The creators of the show are Julia Smith and script editor Tony Holland. The name Walford is both a street in Dalston where Tony Holland lived and a blend of Walthamstow and Stratford,

the areas of Greater London where the creators were born. The bulk of filming takes place at the BBC Elstree Centre in Borehamwood. Off set locations have included Amsterdam, Ireland, Milan, Portugal and Venice. Alan Jeapes and Simon May composed the famous theme tune.

The majority of EastEnders' characters are working-class and feature a culturally diverse cast. EastEnders observes the domestic and professional lives of the people who live and work in fictional Albert Square and its neighbouring streets – Bridge Street, Turpin Road and George Street. Characters are seen in the street market, nightclub, community centre, charity shop, café, wine bar, park, allotments and an assortment of small businesses. Focus is built around the idea of relationships and strong

families, depicting everyday life in the inner city. However, the programme has been criticised by the Commission for Racial Equality, who argued in 2002 that EastEnders was not giving a realistic representation of the East End's 'ethnic make-up'. The programme has since attempted to address these issues. A sari shop was opened and various characters of differing ethnicities were introduced throughout 2006 and 2007, including the Fox family, the Masood's and various background artists.

The show is well known for tackling many controversial and taboo issues previously unseen on television in the UK. EastEnders is the most complained about programme on the BBC. When character Ronnie swapped her newborn baby with Kat Moon's living son, 8,500 complaints were received. However, in contrast, the child abuse storyline with Kat Slater and her uncle Harry saw calls to the National Society for the Prevention of Cruelty to Children (NSPCC) go up by 60%. After an episode featuring domestic abuse, an associated helpline attracted over 2,000 calls in one night.

Storylines have included the cot death of 14-month-old Hassan Osman, Nick Cotton's homophobia, racism and murder of Reg Cox, the rape of Kathy Beale by James Willmott-Brown, Michelle Fowler's teenage pregnancy and Mark Fowler discovering he was HIV positive. The soap opera has also dealt with murder, adoption, abortion, agoraphobia, bipolar, breast cancer, divorce, domestic violence, euthanasia, mixed-race relationships, illiteracy, mugging, prostitution, shoplifting, sexism and schizophrenia. On Christmas Day in 1986, a combined 30.15 million viewers tuned in to see Den Watts hand over divorce papers to wife Angie, the highest rated episode of a soap in British television history. There has been a constant battle in the ratings war and in July 2013 the programme became the third highest rated soap behind rivals Emmerdale and Coronation Street.

The first central families were the Beales and Fowlers, which included Pauline Fowler (Wendy Richard), her husband Arthur Fowler (Bill Treacher) and children Mark Fowler and Michelle Fowler. Living nearby was Pauline's twin brother Pete Beale, his wife Kathy Beale and their teenage son Ian Beale. Pauline and Pete's mother Lou Beale lived with Pauline and her family. Dot and Ethel were also firm favourites. Additional families have joined the cast and each have been central to dramatic plots, the Watts, Mitchells, Slater and Brannings for example.

Tony Holland is said to have drawn on his own family experiences to create characters. There have been a steady stream of strong female characters: Lou Beale, Bianca Butcher, Pauline Fowler, Mo Harris, Pat Butcher, Peggy Mitchell, Zainab Masood and Cora Cross. The many female characters over the years have often been central to the plots, most having to deal with danger and adversity: Angie Watts, Kathy Beale, Sharon Rickman, Pat Butcher, Denise Fox, Tanya Cross, Sue Osman, Little Mo Mitchell, Laura Beale, Lisa Fowler, Tiffany Mitchell, Kat Moon, Stacey Branning and Ronnie Mitchell are all examples of these. Tough male personalities balance the cast and include Den Watts, Phil Mitchell, Grant Mitchell, Jack Branning, Max Branning, Joey Branning and Michael Moon.

The iconic male villains include Archie Mitchell, Nick Cotton, Trevor Morgan, James Wilmot-Brown, and Yusef Khan. The female equivalents have been Cindy

Beale, Janine Butcher and Lucy Beale. Another recurring male character seen in EastEnders is the 'loser' or 'soft touch'. These are men, often comically under the thumb of their female counterparts, which have included Arthur Fowler, Ricky Butcher, Lofty Holloway and Billy Mitchell. Other recurring character types that have appeared throughout the serial are 'cheeky-chappies' Pete Beale, Alfie Moon and Garry Hobbs, 'lost girls' such as

Mary Smith, Donna Ludlow and Mandy Salter and delinquents such as Mandy Salter, Stacey Branning, Jay Mitchell and Lola Pearce. The cockney 'wide boys' or 'wheeler dealers' have always been firm favourites and include Frank Butcher, Alfie Moon, Kevin Wicks, Darren Miller and Fatboy.

Over the years EastEnders has typically featured a number of elderly residents, who are used to show vulnerability, nostalgia, stalwart-like attributes and are sometimes used for comedic purposes. The original elderly residents included Lou Beale, Ethel Skinner and Dot Cotton. Over the years they have been joined by the likes of Mo Butcher, Jules Tavernier, Marge Green, Nellie Ellis, Jim Branning, Patrick Trueman, Cora Cross and Rose Cotton.

The show has also become known for the return of characters after they have left the series. Sharon Rickman returned in August 2012 for her seventh stint on the show and Den Watts returned 14 years after he was believed to have died. Speaking extras, including Tracey the barmaid (who has been in the show since the first episode in 1985) have made appearances throughout the show's duration, without being the focus of any major storyline. The character of Nick Cotton gained a reputation for making constant exits and returns since the programme's first episode.

Despite the high cast turnover, several cast members have remained with the show for an extended period of time; Sharon Watts and Ian Beale are the two remaining original characters in the soap. Ian Beale is the only character to have appeared continuously from the first episode and is the longest serving character in EastEnders.

EastEnders remains topical, referencing current events in episodes. The show covered the general election of 1987, featuring all the major parties. During the 2006 FIFA World Cup, actors filmed short scenes following the tournament's events which were later edited into the programme. Last-minute scenes have also been recorded to commemorate historic moments such as, Barack Obama's election victory in 2008, the death of Michael Jackson in 2009, Andy Murray's Wimbledon victory in 2013 and the birth of Prince George of Cambridge.

EastEnders has also been praised for its portrayal of characters with disabilities, including Adam Best (spina bifida), Noah Chambers (deaf), Jean Slater and her daughter Stacey (bipolar disorder), Janet Mitchell and Craig Moon (Down's syndrome) and Jim Branning (stroke).

For its 25th anniversary in February 2010, EastEnders featured a live broadcast.

The show is broadcast around the world and is very popular with HM Forces and their families stationed overseas, tuning in via the British Forces Broadcasting Service.

EastEnders has won six BAFTA Awards, as well as ten National Television Awards for 'Most Popular Serial Drama' and ten awards for 'Best Soap' at the British Soap Awards. It has also won eight TV Quick and TV Choice Awards for 'Best Soap', six TRIC Awards for 'Soap of The Year' and four Royal Television Society Awards for 'Best Continuing Drama'.

Eldorado

A British soap, filmed entirely abroad and run for just one year, starting on 6th July 1992 and ending on 9th July 1993, with a total of 156 episodes. Set in the fictional town of Los Barcos on the Costa del Sol in Spain, Eldorado was based around the lives of British and European expatriates and was created by Julia Smith and Tony Holland. The original title was proposed as 'Little England' but this was deemed too provincial.

The BBC wanted a hit soap to compete with ITV's Emmerdale and Coronation Street. A high-profile advertising campaign was initiated on television, radio and in the press. A host of journalists were flown to Spain to record the much-hyped launch. The ratings war began immediately with ITV broadcasting a special one hour edition of Coronation Street at the same time as Eldorado's debut show. The BBC was confident that scandal, sun, sea and sangria would prove immensely popular with viewers and become the perfect antidote to the drab lives and scenery in EastEnders and Coronation Street.

The first episode opened with the controversial story of a middle-aged man, Bunny (Roger Walker) returning from the UK with a 17-year-old bride, Fizz (Kathy Pitkin). Eldorado ended as implausibly as it began, Marcus Tandy (Jesse Birdsall) cheating death as his car exploded, boarding his boat and sailing off into the distance with his girlfriend Pilar (Sandra Sandri).

Eldorado is mainly remembered as an embarrassing failure for the BBC and the single biggest television flop. Critics were harsh from the start and a combination

of untrained actors, foreign dialogue without subtitles and acoustic problems spelled the beginning of the end for Eldorado.

A purpose built site in the hills near Marbella provided the backdrop to the doomed 1992 serial. The production budget exceeded 10 million pounds for the entire year. Much of the money was spent on creating the set, which was intended to imitate the sunshine and simplicity of life in the successful Australian soaps. After the programme was axed by the newly appointed BBC controller Alan Yentob, the site was abandoned. It became a hotel complex called Hotel Ciudad Del Cine for a short time, but that enterprise failed too and Eldorado is now a ghost town, the sunshine soap a distant memory.

Emergency – Ward 10

Emergency – Ward 10 was a British television series, was first shown on the 19th February 1957 for a run of ten years. The series was an immediate success and over one million viewers tuned in to watch the first episode. The closing signature tune titled 'Silks and Satins' by Peter Yorke was a stock library track and therefore could be used by any production company. As a result of this, the piece was often heard on Prisoner: Cell Block H.

Set in the fictitious surroundings of Oxbridge General Hospital, the programme was not intended to exceed six episodes and was originally called 'Calling Nurse Roberts'. The show in fact went on to become one of the nation's best loved programmes. The series concentrated on the lives of the men and women who staffed the hospital and was also British television's first soap set in the workplace. The doctors' white coats were actually yellow in order to prevent on-screen camera flare. Because the production was made and shown in monochrome, viewers were none the wiser.

Although the episodes contained plenty of drama, there was a very low mortality rate and patient deaths were strictly limited to five per year. The medical series was demure in comparison to today's standards but it courted extensive debate in 1964 with its portrayal of an interracial relationship between surgeon Louise Mahler (Joan Hooley) and Doctor Giles Farmer (John White) and showed the first ever on-screen interracial kiss.

More positive press came via The British Medical Association who congratulated the show for calming

people's dread of hospitals. In 1962 the Minister of Health, Enoch Powell, applauded the show for its constructive influence on the public by reinforcing the importance of immunisation.

Many stars were generated from the series: Nurse Carole Young (Jill Browne), Australia's Charles 'Bud' Tingwell starred in the series as surgeon Alan 'Digger' Dawson and achieved pin-up status. Other key cast members included Dr. Simon Forrester (Frederick Bartman), Dr. Whittaker (Robert MacLeod), Nurse Pat Roberts (Rosemary Miller), Staff

Nurse Amy Williams (Sonia Fox), Porter (Douglas Ives) and Mrs Anderson (Noel Hood).

The long list of patients who received treatment within 'EW10's' walls included Ian Hendry, Joanna Lumley, John Alderton, Dandy Nicholls, Paul Darrow and Albert Finney.

'Life in Emergency Ward 10' was a 1958 full-length feature film. After the show was cancelled, many viewers complained. 'General Hospital' was created as a bid to try and revive the series but it had far less impact on viewers.

Emmerdale

Emmerdale Farm was first broadcast on the 16th October 1972. It was a British soap opera set in Emmerdale, a fictional village in the Yorkshire Dales, originally known as Beckindale. The programme was later named Emmerdale in 1989 and an average eight million viewers watched each episode. Kevin Laffan created the show and it is the UK's second oldest television soap opera. The title sequences for very early episodes of the soap were filmed at Arncliffe in Littondale and where it is understood the series derived its title – 'Amerdale' being the ancient Norse name for Littondale. The original theme tune was composed by Tony Hatch.

The basic foundation of Emmerdale began with the Sugden family, siblings Jack (Andrew Burt), Joe (Frazer Hines) and Peggy (Jo Kendall), their farm and characters in a nearby village. Their father Jacob Sugden was buried in the first episode. As the show progressed from a minor daytime rural drama, into one of the UK's most major soaps, more families were introduced: The Bartons, Dingles, Kings, Maceys, Windsors, Sharmas and the Tates, originally of Home Farm. There are still some Sugdens in the village: Jack Sugden's widow Diane Sugden and his two children Andy Sugden and Victoria Sugden; Andy's children with Debbie Dingle, Sarah and Jack and Andy's ex-wife Katie Sugden.

On the 30th December 1993, Emmerdale attracted its highest ever audience of over 18 million when a plane crashed into the village, killing four villagers. This led to the villagers deciding to have the village name changed from Beckindale to Emmerdale to help recover

from the plane crash. The story gained a lot of press and audience attention. The plot line, however, caused a great deal of controversy due to the similarity to the Lockerbie disaster; it was aired near to the time of the fifth anniversary of that disaster.

Emmerdale celebrated its 40th Anniversary in 2012 and became the first ever soap to stage a live outside broadcast; a new Woolpack pub was built for the live episode. The one hour instalment featured the murder of Carl King, two weddings and two births. Emmerdale entered a new era in 2013 as actor Richard Thorp who played Alan Turner died. At the time, he was the longest serving Emmerdale actor, playing his character for 31 years. Christopher Chittell has played Eric Pollard for 28 years.

Some of the most acclaimed and dramatic storylines include the death of the Skilbeck twins, Pat Sugden's car crash, Sarah's kidnapping, Viv Hope

killed in a village fire, a plane crash in 1993, the Home Farm siege in 1994, the Post Office robbery in 1998, the bus crash in 2000, the storm in 2003/4, the King's House collapse in 2006, the death of Tom King in 2006, the Sugden's house fire in 2007, the attack of Cain Dingle in 2011 and the Woolpack siege in 2013.

The death of Tom King heralded an entirely new angle for soap opera viewers; the whole storyline was fully interactive, allowing viewers the opportunity of becoming super sleuths to help solve the crime and use an online portal. The viewers were taken inside the show and had direct online interaction with the storyline. Secrecy was paramount, even the cast and crew didn't know who the killer was.

The houses of the Emmerdale set are timber-framed structures covered in stone cladding. The village is built on green belt land, so all the buildings are classed as 'temporary structures'. Location footage is carried out in other areas of the City of Leeds, and other locations in West Yorkshire, such as the fictional market town of Hotten, which is actually shot in Otley. There have been four farms featured in Emmerdale throughout its run.

Families

Families was an early nineties show that had a unique UK- Australian crossover angle. The series followed the lives of the Thompson family in England and the Stevens family based in Sydney Australia. The Thompson's lived in England in the fictional market town of Westbury. The first episode was aired on the 23rd April 1990, the last in August 1993 and encompassed a total of 324 episodes. Produced at Granada TV studios in Manchester, Families was created by Kay Mellor. The theme music was composed by Matthew Scott.

This twice-weekly drama began with the story of Cheshire businessman Mike Thompson (Malcolm Stoddard) hitting a midlife crisis. The pressures of everyday life resulted in Mike leaving his wife Sue (Morag Hood) and family in England and running away to reunite with his first love,

Diana Stevens (Briony Behets) in Australia. Mike's family remained in Cheshire and fought to keep the business going whilst he enjoyed life in Sydney. Diana Stevens and Mike Thompson had a past that reconnected their two families. Their story was the foundation for the series until 1992 when the Bannerman family were introduced to the series. The Bannermans moved into the Thompsons' Cheshire mansion and became the new central family on the show.

Key character Andrew, Diana's eldest son moved to England and fell in love with Mike's daughter Amanda. It materialised that Mike was actually Andrew's father also, which caused heartache for both families.

The Harvey family arrived later and became central characters. Charles (Terence Harvey), his wife Isabelle (Helen Bourne) and their children, Simon

(Thomas Russell), teenager Matthew (Oliver Milburn). Fiona Lewis (Claire Marchionne) also appeared in the show and turned out to be Charles' mistress. Jude Law was a regular cast member for two years as Nathan Thompson.

The show was unusual for a daytime soap, regularly tackling subjects that at the time would have been considered contentious for primetime audiences. Storylines included murder, suicide, incest, drugs, adultery, prostitution, mental health problems and homosexuality. It also contained some strong language and scenes of a sexual nature, all of which were screened just before children's television started after school time.

The show was decommissioned to make way for daytime repeats of Coronation Street and Emmerdale. A dramatic feature-length finale saw a birth, a possible suicide and a large and unexpected inheritance.

Family Affairs

Set in the imaginary west London suburb of Charnam, London W15, Family Affairs was the first show broadcast on Channel Five when it launched in March 1997 and the soap opera ran until the 30th December 2005 totalling 2285 episodes.

The production pace of Family Affairs was fast and sometimes chaotic. The series was filmed as a timeshare at a studio in Merton, south London along with the police drama The Bill. The words 'Sun Hill' were removed from the front of the police station for the Family Affairs filming.

Family Affairs had a diverse cast and the main characters were based around the middle-class Hart family: parents Chris (Ian Ashpitel), Annie (Liz Crowther) and their four children, Duncan (Rocky Marshall), Duncan's twin, Holly (Sandra Huggett), Melanie (Cordelia Bugeja) and Jamie (Michael Cole). Another key character was Pete Callan (David Easter), the villainous pub landlord who had endless questionable dealings. Other regulars at the start of the show included Yasmin Green (Ebony Thomas) with her relationship sagas and gossip fuelled Sadie Hargreaves Lloyd (Barbara Young). The usual meeting place for characters was at The Lock, bar and restaurant.

The show's five weekly episodes gave an opportunity for more gritty and slow-burning storylines. The soap also relied heavily on family based storylines and marital upsets. Other plots involved murder, rape, prostitution, blackmail, use, incest, kidnapping and abortion. Family Affairs was often acclaimed for its constant inclusion of minority groups and was praised for its treatment and

integration of characters from ethnic minorities.

During a series revamp in 1999 The Warrington Family moved into Stanley Street and the entire Hart family was killed; a fallen candle caused a gas explosion on a boat. A particular series highlight was the story of Tanya Franks who fell in love with the surrogate mother of her baby. A Family Affairs storyline, in which a couple learned that a family friend had abused their daughter, earned the show two British Soap Awards. Ratings remained low but consistent up until the final episode.

General Hospital

General Hospital is the longest-running American soap opera and it premiered on the 1st April 1963. The show was created by husband-and-wife team, Frank and Doris Hursley. The show has mainly been filmed in Hollywood since its inception and the theme music was composed by Jack Urbont.

The series originally focused on the medical staff at Port Charles' General Hospital and starred John Beradino as Dr. Steve Hardy and Emily McLaughlin as Nurse Jessie Brewer. Jessie's turbulent marriage to Dr. Phil Brewer (Roy Thinnes) was the centre of many early storylines. In 1964, Audrey March (Rachel Ames) a flight attendant and sister of Nurse Lucille (Lucille Wall) was the woman who won Steve's heart. The series then branched out and focused more on the people and families of the town of Port Charles.

The current families on the show include the bickering and prosperous Quartermaine family, the notorious Corinthos family, the middle-class Scorpio/Jones family, the noble Cassadine family, and the adventurous Spencer family. Rachel Ames is the longest serving actress on an ABC soap opera, having been continuously on the show from 1964 to 2007. The soap opera is also known for its high-profile celebrity guest stars which have included Roseanne Barr, James Franco and Elizabeth Taylor.

From 1979 to 1988, General Hospital had more viewers than any other daytime soap opera. It rose to the top of the ratings in the early 1980s largely due to the immensely popular 'supercouple' Luke and Laura. Their 1981 wedding attracted

30 million viewers, the highest-rated hour in American soap opera history. General Hospital was also praised for the love story of teenagers Stone Cates (Michael Sutton) and Robin Scorpio (Kimberly McCullough). After a struggle that lasted throughout most of 1995, Stone died from AIDS at the age of 19 and his death was followed by 17-year-old Robin having to deal with being HIV-positive as a result of their relationship.

During the 1980s, the series featured several high-profile action, adventure and science fiction-based storylines. Location shooting at sites including Mount Rushmore in South Dakota, Niagara Falls, Grand Ole Opry in Nashville, Tennessee, Atlantic City, New Jersey, Big Bear and Avalon (Catalina Island), California and San Antonio, Texas are some that propelled the storylines.

The show celebrated its 50th anniversary on the 1st April 2013. Several storylines reminiscent of iconic story arcs of the past were created and popular characters returned to the show in order to commemorate the 50th anniversary of the series in 2013.

In 1972, General Hospital generated a primetime spin-off with the same name in the United Kingdom and it ran until 1979. The UK series General Hospital did not feature any characters from the American show but was modelled on its format.

General Hospital has had many famous fans, including Wayne Gretzky and his wife Janet Jones, The Sopranos actor Vincent Pastore, skier Kristi Leskinen, actor Jason Gray-Stanford, motocross rider Mike Metzger and singer Billy Currington. Princess Diana was a devout fan of the show and went as far as to send two bottles of Bollinger champagne to Anthony Geary and Genie Francis in time for Luke and Laura's 1981 wedding. Geary turned his into a lamp.

General Hospital holds the record for the most Daytime Emmy Awards for Outstanding Drama Series, with 11 wins.

ERAL HOSPITAL

Grange Hill

Grange Hill began in 1978 on BBC1 and ended its run after thirty years in 2008; it was created by Phil Redmond. The series was originally going to be called 'Grange Park'. The first theme tune was called 'Chicken Man' and was composed by Alan Hawkshaw.

The drama was centred on the fictional, north London comprehensive school of Grange Hill and followed the lives of the students as they progressed through school.

The series caused extensive controversy for its plucky portrayal of school life. One of the most famous storylines was that of Zammo McGuire (Lee MacDonald) and his addiction to heroin. The 1986 cast released the single 'Just Say No' in connection with Zammo's story. The decision to tackle the subject of rape upset some parents and many complaints were received. The teachers also began to feature in the narrative with a look into their personal lives, which provoked more complaints, especially when Grange Hill broke new ground by the inclusion of a gay teacher, Mr Brisley. There were a total of nine head teachers at Grange Hill, with Mrs McClusky as possibly the most memorable.

Other favourite characters from the early days included Tucker (Todd Carty), Trisha Yates (Michelle Herbert), Douglas 'Pogo' Patterson (Peter Moran), Suzanne Ross (Suzanne Tully), Roland 'Roly' Browning (Erkan Mustafa) and the comedic duo Gonch (John Holmes) and Hollo (Bradley Sheppard). One of the most outstanding episodes was the (aborted) trip to France, where Tucker and Al tried to get Tommy across the

border as a stowaway, but a French customs official discovered them. The three were so popular with viewers that, when they left the school, they starred in their own spin-off, Tucker's Luck (1983–1985). Two former pupils became staff members of Grange Hill in the show's final years: Taylor Mitchell, who became assistant caretaker and Kathy McIlroy, who was appointed as a liaison officer to primary schools.

The series celebrated its 20th anniversary with the introduction of sinister Scottish bully Sean Pearce (Iain Robertson), who carried a knife and slashed the face of a classmate. Cast member Laura Sadler, who was heavily involved in this storyline, died after falling out of a building in June 2003; four years earlier her Grange Hill character Judi Jeffreys was killed after slipping and falling out of the window of a burning storeroom in the school. The show received praise for the inclusion of characters with disabilities: Denny Roberts (Lisa Hammond), who had dwarfism and Rachel Burns (Francesca Martinez) who had cerebral palsy.

The gates to Grange Hill were finally closed on Monday 15th September 2008 with a return appearance by Todd Carty, in which Tucker persuaded his nephew Togger Johnson not to give up on school as he had done.

Holby City

Holby City is a medical based soap drama that premiered on the 12th January 1999. Viewers follow life on the medical wards at Holby City General Hospital, focusing on staff and patients. The series was created by Tony McHale and Mal Young as a spin-off from Casualty. Mal Young wanted the crossover programme to explore the journey of patients after they left the frenetic accident and emergency department. Both shows are set in Holby in the fictional county of Wyvern.

At the inception of Holby City, the cast focused on just 11 main characters, all have since left the show. This cast encompassed consultants Anton Meyer (George Irving), Muriel McKendrick (Phyllis Logan), registrars Nick Jordan (Michael French) and Kirstie Collins (Dawn McDaniel), senior house officer Victoria Merrick (Lisa Faulkner), ward sisters Karen Newburn (Sarah Preston) and Julie Bradford (Nicola Stephenson), nurse practitioner Jasmine Hopkins (Angela Griffin), senior staff nurse Ray Sykes (Ian Curtis), theatre sister Ellie Sharpe (Julie Saunders) and ward clerk Paul Ripley (Luke Mably). The shows longest serving character was Chrissie Williams as portrayed by Tina Hobley who was with the show for 12 years from 2001 to 2013 and appeared in more than 350 episodes. Holby City and Casualty have occasionally aired linked storylines: a romance between Holby City's Ben Saunders (David Paisley) and Casualty's Tony Vincent (Lee Warburton), and Casualty's Charlie Fairhead (Derek Thompson) was operated on by Holby City's Elliot Hope after suffering a heart

attack

The present cast now features 16 key cast members: CEO and director of surgery Guy Self (John Michie), deputy CEO and consultant Serena Campbell (Catherine Russell), Director of Nursing Colette Sheward (Louise Delamere), consultants Ric Griffin (Hugh Quarshie), Elliot Hope (Paul Bradley) and Jac Naylor (Rosie Marcel), specialist registrars Sacha Levy (Bob Barrett), Mo Effanga (Chizzy Akudolu) and Raf di Lucca (Joe McFadden), CT2 doctor Harry Tressler (Jules Knight), F2 doctor Arthur Digby (Rob Ostlere), F1 doctors Dominic Copeland (David Ames) and Zosia March (Camilla Arfwedson), clinical nurse manager and transplant coordinator Jonny Maconie (Michael Thomson), staff nurse Mary-Claire Carter (Niamh McGrady) and Healthcare Assistant Adele Effanga (Petra Letang).

Each episode of Holby City costs in the region of £370,000 to produce in comparison to EastEnders at £130,000 per episode and Casualty at £450,000. Holby City has come under fire from critics who believe the production costs are a poor use of licence payer's fees. Holby City counteract the accusation by the fact that it is a high-volume, year-round production, it therefore has relatively low production costs. Set-up costs can be spread over many years and standing sets can be repeatedly re-used, which is not the case for shorter series or one-off dramas.

Holby City has attracted comparisons to other medical dramas, often adverse, but the programme does also receives commendation. The Royal National Institute for Deaf People (RNID) spoke in favour of an episode which coincided with 'Learn To Sign Week', with roles played by deaf actors, featuring characters communicating through British Sign Language. Jill Berry, president of the Girls' Schools Association and head teacher at the Dame Alice Harpur School in Bedford, cited medical dramas such as Holby City as an inspiring force in increasing numbers of female students deciding to pursue careers in medicine. The series employs a team of researchers to ensure medical accuracy and utilises surgeons from different disciplines to check scripts. Cast members are taught to perform basic medical procedures and are given the opportunity to spend

time on real hospital wards for research. George Irving observed coronary artery bypass surgery performed at Papworth and Middlesex Hospital in preparation for his role as Anton Meyer. One medical advisor was given a cameo role in the

series as an orthopaedic surgeon and another as recovery nurse.

Holby City has featured a number of famous guest stars including Emma Samms, Antonio Fargas, Anita Dobson, Peter Bowles, Susannah York, Johnny Briggs, Richard Briers, Eric Sykes, Phill Jupitus, Kieron Dyer, Denise Welch, Sheridan Smith and David Soul.

The series won a BAFTA in 2008 for Best Continuing Drama, and consistently draws over 4 million viewers.

Hollyoaks

This British soap opera was first broadcast on Channel 4 on the 23rd October 1995. The programme is set in a fictional suburb of Chester called Hollyoaks and it is filmed at studios in Abbey Road, Liverpool. The village is purpose built and some parts were once used for the Brookside set. Hollyoaks was originally devised by Phil Redmond and quickly established a substantial fan base where it is viewed as a vibrant, modern young person's soap. The theme music has been changed six times to date.

Beginning with a cast of just seven major characters in 1995, the serial now has approximately 50 main cast members. Many characters are students and there is an assortment of key families who remain central to various plots. At the start these were The Cunningham, Osborne,

McQueen and Ashworth families. Three new families were introduced in 2010: The Sharpe, Costello and O'Connor families. The Savage family replaced the Sharpes before they were joined by the Kanes, Roscoe and Lomax family units. Nick Pickard who portrays Tony Hutchinson, is the only cast member to have appeared consecutively from the show's inception.

Over the course of the show's history, Hollyoaks has dealt with a number of contentious storylines. The show is very popular with a young audience and is seen as an ideal tool to convey cautionary messages and raise awareness of serious issues. A telephone helpline is usually displayed after a story that may have affected viewers. An episode screened in 2007 featured a story relating to carbon monoxide poisoning that alerted a

HOLLYOAKS

#Hollyoaks

viewer to recognise the similarity of her own symptoms; she then received life saving medical attention. Storylines that the soap has dealt with also include drug addiction, murder, arson, hit-and-run, abortion, suicide, homelessness, financial problems, interracial relationships, racism, religion, bisexuality, homosexuality, Gender Identity Disorder, bullying, homophobia, sexual confusion, alcoholism, rape, incest, cancer, male rape, child abuse and domestic violence.

Keen to portray realistic themes that echo the modern world, Hollyoaks will often collaborate with expert services. Producers teamed up with Channel 4 Education's Battlefront to work responsibly on a storyline involving underage sex between characters Finn O'Connor and Amber Sharpe that resulted in Amber's pregnancy. Hollyoaks was the first British television programme to tackle the issue of homosexual domestic violence, with Brendan Brady (Emmett J.'Scanlan) and Ste Hay (Kieron Richardson). An episode titled 'Enjoy The Ride' won critical acclaim in which four regular characters were killed: Rhys Ashworth (Andrew Moss), and three sixth form students, Maddie Morrison (Scarlett Bowman), Neil Cooper (Tosin Cole) and Jono (Dylan Llewellyn). The show has a very high turnover of actors and it is not uncommon for many actors to be written out in quick succession. In October 2013 the show aired Hollyoaks 'The Blast', in which five main characters were killed off.

Hollyoaks is broadcast in numerous countries and is very popular in New Zealand, where it ranks far higher in the ratings than EastEnders. The programme is renowned for striving to be a soap that remains relevant to the audience. In November 2010, a special scene was filmed for an episode airing on the 19th November 2010 featuring Myra McQueen (Nicole Barber-Lane) that referred to the engagement of Prince William and Kate Middleton.

Several authentic acts have also performed on Hollyoaks: The Alphites, Darius Campbell, The Saturdays, McFly and Hosen Brass. Hollyoaks has won 24 British Soap Awards, 11 Inside Soap Awards, 1 TRIC Award and 1 National Television Award. In 2013, the soap won its very first Best Soap Award at the Digital Spy Soap Awards.

Other notable characters include Sol Patrick, Justin Burton, Ste Hay, Michaela McQueen, Amy Barnes, villains such as Rob Hawthorne, Toby Mills, Andy Holt, Niall Rafferty, Silas Blissett, Brendan Brady, 'bad boy' club owners Scott Anderson, Trevor Royle and Warren Fox, vixens such as Cindy Cunningham, Clare Devine and Louise Summers, businessmen such as Tony Hutchinson, Gordon Cunningham and Neville Ashworth and sweethearts such as Mandy Richardson, Carmel Valentine and Hannah Ashworth.

Hollyoaks' is also known for its 'sexy' characters including Dodger Savage, Mercedes Fisher, Carmel Valentine, Sarah Barnes, Annalise Appleton, Calvin Valentine and John Paul McQueen. Characters such as Brendan Brady, Mitzeee, Craig Dean, Hannah Ashworth and Jacqui McQueen are known as some of the most popular characters in the show's history, while characters like Gabby Sharpe, Will Savage and Govinda Roy have been widely criticised. Hollyoaks also featured Kelly-Marie Stewart as Hayley Ramsey, the first character with a disability to be part of the cast.

Home And Away

Home and Away is a hit Australian series that has been in production since January 1988. The series is set in the small coastal town of imaginary Summer Bay and production filming for the beach scenes takes place at Palm Beach. Interiors for the show are filmed at Seven Sydney's Epping studios and the Australian Technology Park. The series was created by Alan Bateman and it first went on air on the 17th January 1988. The theme tune's lyrics have remained the same since the pilot episode.

The programme was going to be called 'The Refuge', but it was considered unfriendly. The classic Australian soap depicts the trials and tribulations of the town's residents. There is an underlying and ever present message that the show conveys: a community functions best when everyone works together.

In the beginning, the programme was centered on the Stewart and Fletcher families. Pippa (Vanessa Downing) and Tom Fletcher (Roger Oakley) and the children they fostered: Frank Morgan (Alex Papps), Carly Morris (Sharyn Hodgson), Steven Matheson (Adam Willits), Lynn Davenport (Helena Bozich) and Sally Keating (Kate Ritchie). The character Alf Stewart has lived in Summer Bay for 22 years.

One of the first notorious stories was in relation to the rape of Carly Morris, which critics felt was inappropriate for the pre-watershed time slot. Over the years, however, Home and Away has continued to deal with some very contentious issues. While the show has had a number of light-hearted or comical storylines, there have also been a number of storylines concerned with more adult themes

Home and Away

including domestic violence, bullying (inside and outside of school), gambling addiction, teenage pregnancy, racism, sexual assault, drug dependency, adultery, wrongful imprisonment, suicide, murder, homosexuality, incest and child abuse.

A seemingly out-of-character story was that of Ailsa Stewart being exposed as a murderess who had killed her abusive first husband. Other storylines include the more common soap opera narratives of births, deaths, marriages and the reappearance of long-lost family members. An early story featured the unlikely union

of humourless Donald Fisher as the father of wayward Bobby Simpson. Home and Away is one of the most complained about shows on Australian television. In March 2009, it was alleged that the Seven Network agreed to censor a scene with a lesbian kiss, after pressure from religious groups. More upset was caused when ghostly appearances in Summer Bay were used to help characters move on physically or mentally. One of the most notorious was when Bobby's head appeared in Ailsa's fridge as a result of her nervous breakdown and served as a prompt for Ailsa to seek professional help.

The most memorable characters from the soap opera include Alf Stewart (Ray Meagher) who has been honoured in the naming of Stewart's Point and his catchphrase 'You flamin' mongrels'. Sally Fletcher (Kate Ritchie) joined the cast when she was eight years old. Kate won a Silver Logie for Best Actress and a Golden Logie for Favourite Television Personality at the Australian 'Oscars' in 2007. School Principal Donald Fisher (Norman Coburn), was known to students at Summer Bay High as Flathead. When he left, the farewell sequence in the school hall showed how deeply woven into Summer Bay society he had become. Pippa Fletcher (Vanessa Downing from 1988 to 1990, and Debra Lawrence from 1990 onwards) was the matriarch of Summer Bay for the first ten years of the programme. Pippa was married to Tom who died from a heart attack. Pippa then lost her second husband Michael during a flood. Sally named her daughter Pippa in recognition of the woman she had always seen as her mother.

Many of the youngest actors have learnt their craft on the set of Home and Away before moving onto other successful projects. Dannii Minogue,

Naomi Watts, Heath Ledger, Julian McMahon, Craig McLachlan and Melissa George are all good examples of this. Isla Blair, who played Shannon, has become very famous and also went on to marry Sacha Baron Cohen.

Guest appearances have been made by Michael Palin, Kostya Tszyu the boxer, Ian Thorpe the world-famous swimmer, Lleyton Hewitt, John Farnham, the singer from 'The Voice' and pop group Atomic Kitten.

Home and Away has been well received in the UK, Ireland, France and New Zealand. It is the most successful programme in the history of the Logies and has earned a total of 38 Logie Awards to date.

Howard's Way

BBC1 launched the new Sunday evening series Howard's Way on the 1st September 1985, which was a story depicting the turbulent lives of a South Coast sailing community. It ran for six seasons and was one of the biggest television hits of the decade. The original working title for the series was 'The Boatbuilders', but this was rejected as it sounded too much like a documentary series. Howard's Way was created and produced by Gerard Glaister and Allan Prior. The theme music was composed by Simon May and performed by his orchestra. Marti Webb reached number 13 in 1986 with 'Always There', the lyrical version of the theme tune.

Dubbed 'Dallas on Sea', Howards' Way was the BBC's answer to the glossy American super-soaps of the 1980s with wealth, aspirations and glamour. Set in the fictional town of Tarrant, the spectacular location filming was set along the River Hamble, the Solent and Hampshire coastline. All the interior scenes were shot in the BBC's Pebble Mill studios in Birmingham. More extensive location filming took place in Guernsey, Malta and Gibraltar.

The show follows the fortunes of Tom Howard (Maurice Colbourne) who invested his life savings into The Mermaid Boatyard. Jack Rolfe (Glyn Owen) ran the boatyard with his daughter Avril (Susan Gilmore). Tom's wife Jan (Jan Harvey) follows her dream into the world of high fashion, opening a marine boutique named Periplus with entrepreneur Ken Masters (Stephen Yardley). The Howards' marriage collapsed but their children Leo and Lynne (played by Edward Highmore and Tracey Childs) became the male and female heartthrobs of the programme. Other regulars at the

start were devious millionaire businessman Charles Frere (Tony Anholt) and the affluent but discontented Urquhart family.

Plots revolved around countless intertwined affairs, passionate liaisons and cutting-edge business enterprise. Tom and Jack are embroiled in conflict and melodramatic storylines were plentiful. Lynne Howard was seduced by the ruthless Charles Frere that resulted in a serious accident and cliffhangers entailed a fatal water-skiing accident, a plane crash and an accident during a powerboat race.

The final episode was broadcast on the 25th November 1990. During the production of the fifth series, lead actor Maurice Colbourne died from a heart attack. Episodes were hurriedly rewritten to explain the character's absence but did not resonate too well with audiences and there followed a steady decline in viewership.

The following actors also made guest appearances in the series: Kathleen Byron, Tony Caunter, Richard Wilson, Bruce Boa, Pamela Salem, Burt Kwouk, James Warwick, Annie Lambert, Clive Wood, Stephen Greif, Andrew Burt and Catherine Schell.

Knots Landing

A spin-off from Dallas, Knots Landing was first screened on the 27th December 1979. The show lasted 14 seasons, ending on the 13th May 1993. The soap opera featured the lives of four married couples living in a cul-de-sac called Seaview Circle, a fictitious coastal suburb of Los Angeles. Knots Landing was created by David Jacobs and Michael Filerman and the theme tune was composed by Jerrold Immel. The series was largely inspired by a 1957 movie 'No Down Payment' and location filming focused around Crystalaire Place in Granada Hills, California.

The foundation for Knots Landing was devised around Ellie Ewing buying Gary (Ted Shackelford) and Val (Joan Van Ark) a house on Seaview Circle, a gift for the couple who had remarried (they remarried three times in total).

The relocation was intended to be a new start for Gary who had battled alcohol addiction. Gary was the black sheep of the Ewing clan and shared none of the business acumen gifted to his brothers Bobby and J.R. The four couples who became the main residents of the famous cul-de-sac were Karen (Michele Lee), Sid (Don Murray), Abby Fairgate (Donna Mills), Laura (Constance McCashin) and Richard Avery (John Pleshette) and newlyweds Ginger (Kim Lankford) and Kenny Ward (James Houghton). Another popular character Lilimae Clements (Julie Harris) joined the show as Valene's mother. Michele Lee was the only cast member to appear in all 344 episodes.

Throughout the series, writers explored several social issues, including rape, illegal and prescription drug abuse, abortion, homelessness, the environment,

illiteracy, the Special Olympics and child abuse. Plots were dramatic and varied, deftly blending the world of escapism and reality and the writing on Knots Landing was always highly acclaimed. Iconic plots consist of Sid's death during an operation, Gary being unjustly imprisoned for the murder of singer Ciji, Val thought her twins were stillborn, but they were actually sold on the black market, Laura died from a brain tumour, Gary and Val's weddings and Val's disappearance/kidnap.

In the two-hour series finale on May 13th 1993, the presumed dead Valene returns to Knots Landing, astounding Gary. There were many guest appearances including Patrick Duffy, Larry Hagman, Charlene Tilton, Helen Hunt, Halle Berry.

Neighbours

Neighbours is an Australian fictional television serial set in Melbourne, Australia. Neighbours went to air for the first time on the 18th March 1985 on Australia's Channel Seven. Eighteen months after its Australian debut, Neighbours was broadcast on the BBC. In 2008 the programme switched to broadcast on Channel 5 due to a huge increase in the fee for screening rights and the BBC felt it was an inappropriate use of licence payer's money (£300 million for an eight-year contract). The theme tune was composed by Tony Hatch and Jackie Trent. Early suggestions for the title were No through Road, One Way Street and The People Next Door.

The show follows the day-to-day lives of a group of families and friends who live in Ramsay Street, a cul-de-sac in the fictitious suburb of Erinsborough. The set of Ramsay Street in reality is a residential cul-de-sac called Pin Oak Court in the suburb of Vermont, Melbourne. Owners of the houses on Pin Oak Court were assured that Neighbours was unlikely to last more than a couple of years and were guaranteed regular payments by Grundy TV in return for the use of their home exteriors. Filming locations outside of Australia have included Kenya, the United States and the UK. An historic location episode saw Susan (Jackie Woodbourne) and Karl Kennedy (Alan Fletcher) taking a ride on the London Eye and being married on a boat on the River Thames.

Neighbours was created by Reg Watson. The idea first started to develop when he was working on Crossroads; he wanted to portray three families who are all friends and all live in a small street.

Neighbours

The theory for Neighbours was to try and combine a mix of the formula used for early years of Coronation Street and Crossroads. The sunny location scenes and the lack of poverty were to contrast with the more grimy shots seen in Coronation Street. Neighbours began with three families: the Ramsays, the Robinsons and the Clarkes.

From humble beginnings, Neighbours has developed into one of the world's most popular television serials. An estimated daily audience reaches in excess of 120 million viewers around the world. On 29th April 2011 in the UK, a specially recorded scene celebrated the wedding of Prince William of Wales to Catherine Middleton.

It has become the longest running drama series in Australian television and the seventh longest running serial drama still on the air in the world. Neighbours has proven to be more popular in the United Kingdom than in Australia. The production team are keen to employ social media and new technology to embrace viewership; Neighbours became the first Australian series to establish Twitter accounts for its characters and the first show available to watch on a free iPhone application.

Storylines frequently focus on family

problems including inter-generational clashes, school problems, romances and domestic issues, as well as many serious problems such as teenage pregnancy, abortion, surrogacy, eating disorders, alcoholism, adultery, drug use, robbery, stalking, kidnapping, murder, and incest. An insight into health issues has also been explored: multiple sclerosis, bipolar disorder and epilepsy.

Significant characters include Jason Donovan (Scott Robinson), Kylie Minogue (Charlene Mitchell), Anne Charleston (Madge), Ian Smith (Harold Bishop), Jim Robinson (Alan Dale), Paul Robinson (Stefan Dennis) and Helen Daniels (Anne Haddy). The show is now a mixture of older characters like Lou Carpenter (Tom Oliver), Toadfish Rebecchi (Ryan Moloney), Karl and Susan Kennedy, as well as newer characters such as the Turner family.

Neighbours has been the launch pad for some of the world's most recognisable artists including Kylie Minogue, Jason Donovan, Guy Pearce, Natalie Imbruglia and Alan Dale, Jesse Spencer, Holly Valance, Delta Goodrem and Sam Clark. Guest appearances have also been made by Russell Crowe, Lily Allen, Matt Lucas, David Walliams and Emma Bunton.

Park Avenue

A daily teletext based soap opera on ITV's ORACLE Teletext service. Park Avenue remains the only soap of its kind in the United Kingdom. The programme was launched on the 1st December 1988 and all 1,445 episodes were written by Robbie Burns. The five o'clock chapters came to an end in 1992 as the service lost its franchise. Park Avenue was set in the fictional town of Parkfield, London. Storylines focused on the lives of the Park Avenue residents. Each episode was scripted across ten pages, with an alternative page number providing a synopsis briefing that allowed viewers to catch up. On occasion, the author wrote character profiles and used teletext-graphics to portray a visual account of a character's appearance. Although Robbie Burns wrote a number of episodes in advance, he was able to make topical additions to storylines; during the 1990 BSE scare, a character decided he would no longer buy beef. Another character became embroiled in a prison riot, which echoed the Strangeways Prison riot and subsequent copycat events in jails across England, Wales and Scotland.

At an age that was pre-internet and social media, Park Avenue was ahead of its time by offering fans an active involvement in the soap. Readers would be invited to vote by phone to decide on story outcomes. Interactive viewers also had a chance to submit entries for story ideas and invent new characters. The programme was very customer centric and offered a service for the purchase of episode printouts; seven episodes cost under £2.50. The

popularity of the show was a recipe that has not been successfully duplicated. ORACLE's successor attempted a recreation with a daily feature called 'Diary of an odd couple', but it only ran for a very brief period.

Pobol y Cwm

The first episode of the Welsh language series was first seen on our screens on the 16th October 1974. Pobol y Cwm, meaning People of the Valley, has been running for over forty years. The show is the most watched programme of the week on the Welsh channel S4C (apart from rugby match broadcasts). The show is the longest running BBC television soap and provides optional subtitles for non-Welsh speakers.

The setting for the show is the fictional village of Cwmderi, in the real Gwendraeth Valley, the heart of the South Wales valleys. Storylines are mostly centred on local residents who often gather at the village pub, Y Deri. Other frequent settings include local businesses, the comprehensive school, Ysgol y Mynach, and a local farm, Penrhewl. There are two other fictional villages close to the valley, Llanarthur and Cwrt Mynach. Filming takes place at Roath Lock studios and location shoots in and around Cardiff.

Gareth Lewis (Meic Pierce) is famed for his long serving and continuous role in a British television soap. Another stalwart cast member was Gwyn Elfyn who played Denzil Rees for almost 28 years. Other well-known faces who have appeared include Ioan Gruffudd, Rachel Thomas, Huw Garmon, Gillian Elisa, Ieuan Rhys, Aneirin Hughes, and Iwan Rheon. Imogen Thomas made a cameo appearance in 2006.

Pobol y Cwm has won three BAFTA awards to date and the 2005 Best Actor award went to Huw Euron. The 1996 BAFTA special award and 1995 Best Actress Award went to Siw Hughes.

Prisoner: Cell Block H

Prisoner; Cell Block H was an Australian soap with cult status and known by several titles. In Canada the title was 'Caged Women' and 'Prisoner' in Australia. British viewers were familiar with the programme as 'Prisoner: Cell block H' to avoid confusion with an existing UK show called 'The Prisoner'. A total of 692 episodes were filmed and broadcast from the 27th February 1979 until the 11th December 1986. The series creator Reg Watson also wrote for Crossroads, The Young Doctors, Sons and Daughters and Neighbours. Allan Caswell wrote the title song 'On the Inside'.

Wentworth Detention Centre showcased life in prison and the private lives of the officers. Filming took place at Nunawading, Melbourne. At the start of series one, two new prisoners, Karen Travers (Peta Toppano) and Lynn Warner (Kerry Armstrong) join 'mother figure' Beatrice Smith (Val Lehman). Travers was convicted of murdering her husband and Warner was convicted of the abduction and attempted murder of a child. The stark surroundings and tough regime are a shock for the new inmates. Karen is mortified to discover the prison doctor is an ex-boyfriend and her life is further complicated by the aggressive harassment of her cellmate Franky Doyle (Carol Burns). 'Queen' Bea Smith (Val Lehman) victimises Lynn by 'accidentally' burning her hand in the laundry. Quieter inmates include 'Mum' Brooks (Mary Ward), Doreen Anderson (Colette Mann) and Lizzie Birdsworth (Sheila Florance).

The prison officers, or 'screws' as they are called by the women, consist of Governor Erica Davidson (Patsy King), Governor Vera Bennett (Fiona Spence) and Officer Meg Jackson (Elspeth Ballantyne).

Storylines primarily concentrated on the lives of the prisoners and prison staff at the maximum-security unit, block H. The themes of the show were often radical, including feminism, homosexuality and social reform. The series examined in detail the way in which women dealt with incarceration and separation from their families and how released inmates often reoffended.

The major themes of the series were the interpersonal associations between the prisoners and their status in the complicated hierarchy. Both fragile friendships and firm bonds developed amongst the inmates, creating a surrogate family to support or devastate their time within prison walls.

A range of themes was incorporated: smuggling, personality clashes amid prisoners, staff politics, strikes, riots, court cases and police investigations. The series also made good use of cliffhangers, often involving dramatic escapes and catastrophes befalling the prison and its inhabitants. The early episodes revealed a violent and hostile environment that ferments within an explosive mix of vicious chaos. During a clash of two inmates who both strive to be the supremo, a prison riot erupts, Meg Jackson is held hostage, her husband, prison psychiatrist Bill Jackson (Don Barker) is stabbed to death by inmate Chrissie Latham (Amanda Muggleton). Another iconic plot was a terrorist raid on the prison in which governor Erica Davidson was shot and wounded. A much milder storyline followed Karen Travers' decision to appeal against her sentence; she was ultimately released from prison and resumed her romantic connection with Dr. Greg Miller. There was a welcome comedic angle for Bea, Lizzie and Doreen, their bid for freedom took place during a pantomime performance of Cinderella and resulted in them being trapped in a collapsed, underground tunnel.

As the original cast left the series, a new influx of prisoners were moved into Wentworth Detention Centre: colossal husband-basher Monica Ferguson (Lesley Baker), disdainful professional criminal Noeline Burke (Jude Kuring), optimistic murderess Roslyn Coulson (Sigrid Thornton), parent Pat O'Connell (Monica Maughan and fresh talent, Deputy governor, Jim Fletcher (Gerard Maguire). Inmate Judy Bryant (Betty Bobbitt) went to great lengths to intentionally get herself imprisoned to be with her girlfriend, scheming drug dealer Sharon Gilmour (Margot Knight).

Another Ferguson joined the cast, corrupt officer – Joan 'The Freak' Ferguson (Maggie Kirkpatrick). Wearing her trademark black leather gloves, she molested prisoners during unofficial 'body searches', profited from illicit dealings and evil trickled

from every aspect of her character. The ongoing bitterness between Bea Smith and Joan Ferguson became a continued thread and peaked during a colossal prison fire. The Great Fire episode ranked highest amongst Prisoner fans. The series became increasingly violent with ever more thrilling storylines intended to grip viewers. However, declining ratings resulted in the series ending on the 5th September 1986.

In 2013 the SoHo television channel began broadcasting the series Wentworth, a current recreation of Prisoner: Cell Block H, focusing on Bea Smith (Danielle Cormack) when she first entered prison. Following the huge popularity of the show in the UK, a successful stage version was produced in 1989, based on the original scripts.

River City

River City is a Scottish television soap opera, first broadcast on the 24th September 2002. It is currently shown on Tuesday evenings on BBC One Scotland, attracting over 500,000 viewers each week.

River City is set in a close-knit Glasgow community. The central focus of the show is the fictional West End district of Shieldinch. River City is filmed in the town of Dumbarton.

River City features the lives of residents and people working in the district of Shieldinch, Glasgow. Characters gather at the pub 'The Tall Ship', bistro, community centre and café. Storylines are built around relationships and families, dealing with family problems, upset and conflict. The show has a great sense of community and characters pull together in times of need and crisis. The central Hamilton family are made up of Malcolm Hamilton, his daughters, Eileen Donachie and Gina Hamilton, and Gina's daughters Ruth Rossi and Joanne Rossi. Other key family groups are the Hendersons, Adams, Mullens and the Murdoch clan.

A variety of storylines have been represented throughout the 12 years and include a serial attacker, prostitution, child pornography, child abduction, kidnap, murder, affairs, illegitimate births and medical plots of alcoholism, HIV and ovarian cancer.

High-profile appearances have been made by Neighbours' star Stefan Dennis, Hollywood's Maurice Roeves and Doctor Who actress Louise Jameson. Cameo appearances have also been made by Lorraine Kelly and Scott Mills.

RIVER CITY
10 years

Santa Barbara

Santa Barbara was an American television soap opera, first broadcast in the United States on NBC on July 30th 1984. The show revolved around the fascinating and tumultuous lives of the prosperous Capwell family of Santa Barbara, California. Key families featured on the soap were the rival Lockridge family and the more unassuming Andrade and Perkins families.

Santa Barbara aired in over 40 countries around the world and was a firm favourite with Ronald and Nancy Reagan.

Memorable plots encompassed the murder of Channing Capwell Jr and almost every major character was accused of the murder. The show was originally ridiculed for appalling dialogue coupled with unsurprising storylines. When a major earthquake hit Santa Barbara, core character Danny Andrade slept through the whole thing. A complete cast revamp guided the show into more pleasing rating figures and the programme managed to achieve critical acclaim. Santa Barbara became famous for its comedic style and innovative writing. Former nun Mary Duvall McCormick (Harley Jane Kozak) was killed by a giant neon letter 'C' falling from a hotel's sign. Another bizarre plot involved Greg Hughes (Paul Johansson) dreaming that Mason and Julia had been abducted by aliens.

The show's popularity in France spun off a storyline in which Eden Capwell (Marcy Walker), Cruz Castillo (A Martinez), Kelly Capwell (Carrington Garland) and Ric Castillo (Peter Love) went to Paris to search after Eden's and Cruz's child.

Santa Barbara won 24 Daytime Emmy Awards and was nominated 30 times for the same award. The show also won 18 Soap Opera Digest Awards. In 1993, the show was cancelled after 2137 episodes had been aired.

Sons And Daughters

Logie Award-winning Australian soap opera Sons and Daughters was created by Reg Watson and produced by the Reg Grundy Organisation. The first episode aired on the 18th January 1982 and the final episode was broadcast in 1987. Sons and Daughters became the highest rated programme in its slot and was the most watched Australian soap of the 1980s. Although popular when screening reached the UK in 1983, the show did not match the viewership in Australia. The theme tune was written by Peter Pinne & Don Battye.

Many storylines were of the standard romantic and domestic variety, with a little crime and a few business scams thrown into the mix. Comedy was sparse and there seemed to be an ever-present ominous undercurrent. Melodrama was combined with affluent and grandiose settings amongst charming rural locations.

A great deal of time and effort went into finding the perfect cast; 550 people were auditioned in Melbourne, Sydney and Brisbane. Prominent characters were members of The Hamilton and Palmer families, and later the Morrells and Armstrongs. The Hamiltons of Sydney were wealthy and influential; the Palmers of Melbourne were average working class. The Hamiltons and Palmers became linked by the distant, secret affair of David Palmer (Tom Richards) and leading lady Patricia Hamilton (Rowena Wallace). The offspring of that affair, twins John Palmer and Angela Hamilton were furtively adopted into the relevant families. Angela Hamilton (Ally Fowler) from Sydney met John by chance who was a fugitive wrongly accused of murder. Their friendship blossomed and they

fell in love, not realising that they were actually siblings, separated at birth 20 years earlier. Further complications followed when David and Patricia met again after 20 years, their infatuation reignited and resulted in David leaving his wife. Later on more wealth arrived in the form of the Morell clan who managed to marry their way into the Hamilton family.

An iconic final episode was screened in Australia on 19th August 1987 .The majority of the characters were ill-fated and left in a perilous position, some involved in a potential deadly disaster.

Take The High Road

ITV created Take the High Road, their first Scottish, daytime soap. Production began in 1982, the conception of Don Houghton and it ran for 23 years. The programme has now developed a cult following. There were four versions of the theme tune; the first version was performed by Silly Wizard.

The soap was set in the fictional village of Glendarroch and was filmed in the genuine village of Luss on the banks of Loch Lomond. The original name for the imaginary estate and village was Glendhu but it was then renamed Glendarroch. The title of the programme was originally 'High Road– Low Road' but was changed to 'Take the High Road. In 1994, the series name was changed once more to just 'High Road'. English audiences in particular loved the panorama, the 'Scottish lochs, hills and purple heather'

feel to the show. Over two million fans tuned in, including the Queen Mother. It was broadcast in Canada and Australia, proving a favourite with ex–pats.

Many of the early scripts were written by Michael Elder, who also made guest appearances in the show. Books by the same name as the show were also produced by him. There were a few themes in Take the High Road, in line with Scottish culture and Protestant religion. It embarked upon many social issues, such as lesbianism, suicide and drug abuse, which was a new approach for Scottish television. Central character Elizabeth Cunningham was the prosperous lady laird who owned the village and adjacent farms.

The show created stars such as Gwyneth Guthrie, playing nuisance Mrs Mack and Jimmy Chisholm. It also

featured actors such as Alan Cumming, Joe McFadden and Gary Hollywood.

When ITV announced the show was to be cancelled, it resulted in public protest. The issue was raised in Parliament under early day motions and the Daily Record newspaper held a protest too. So many objections were received from viewers in England that some ITV regions re-instated the programme. It was finally cancelled on the 27th April 2003 having run for a total of 1,517 episodes.

Nearly every episode has been added to YouTube by Scottish Television, making the series available to viewers worldwide.

The Archers

The world's longest running radio soap opera. The Archers was first broadcast in 1950 on the BBC Light programme, later on BBC Home Service and is now aired on BBC Radio 4. The characters personal and business struggles have kept the nation gripped for over sixty years and the popularity of drama from the heart of the country is even more admired today than it was at the start. More than 5 million radio listeners and over 1 million internet listeners tune into the 12-minute episodes, to be entertained by the residents of the fictional village of Ambridge in the English Midlands. There are six early evening episodes a week and each is repeated the following day at 2pm. Anyone who misses an episode has another chance to catch up during a 75-minute weekend omnibus edition or use BBC iplayer for on-demand replays. More than 20 thousand fans enjoy the interaction offered by The Archers social media profile on Twitter.

The Archers was created by Godfrey Baseley. The original storylines revolved around three farmers: Dan Archer, Walter Gabriel and George Fairbrother. Programme content received mutual input from the Ministry of Agriculture, Fisheries and Food. The Archers was seen as an ideal way of passing information to the farming community on low budget, efficient farming methods and a means to increase productivity after the rationing during and post World War II. Current content deals with all aspects and pressures of modern day rural life.

The theme tune from The Archers is called 'Barwick Green', a maypole dance from the suite 'My Native Heath',

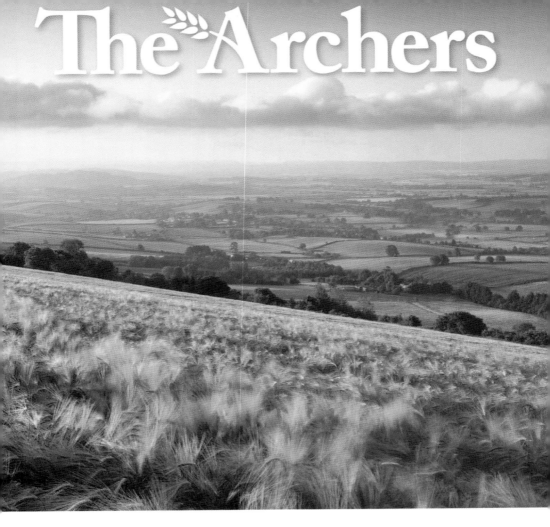

The Archers

composed by Arthur Wood. Student doctors are taught to use the tempo of the tune as the correct rhythm to perform cardiopulmonary resuscitation (CPR). The theme tune was also played during the opening ceremony of the 2012 Olympic Games in recognition of The Archers and British Culture.

Many of the storylines revolve around the title family, the middle-class Archers, who own Brookfield Farm. The farm has been passed down from preceding generations and is now co-owned by three of Phil's four children: David (who manages it with his wife Ruth), Elizabeth and Kenton. One of the most controversial Archers episodes was broadcast on the 22nd September 1955 and featured the death of Grace Archer. Phil and Grace Archer had only been married a few months when tragedy struck. Listeners heard Grace trying to rescue her horse, Midnight, from a raging fire at Brookfield stables and the dramatic, fatal collapse of a beam crushed Grace.

Other key characters include the money orientated Aldridges, the aged and wealthy Woolleys and the ever struggling Grundys. Lynda Snell is a 'new money' pretentious 'incomer' partnered by downtrodden Robert. The Carters are constantly struggling to overcome challenging life hurdles in contrast to the upper class Pargetter's who own Lower Loxley Hall.

The Archers embraces a wide selection of serious social issues including badger culling, genetically modified crops, illicit affairs, rape, drug abuse, inter-racial relationships, divorce and civil partnership. June Spencer (Peggy Woolley) was honoured with a Lifetime Achievement prize in January 2014 at the BBC Audio Drama Awards. Experts have said that her performance during the long-running Alzheimer's storyline has helped to change public attitudes. Minor plots are as popular and the minutiae of everyday occurrences remain a constant thread. A recurring theme has been the resentment of the working-class Grundy family towards the middle-class Archers.

Many famous people have made cameo appearances on the programme: Princess Margaret and the Duke of Westminster appeared in 1984. Camilla, Duchess of Cornwall appeared on 16th February 2011 in support of the National Osteoporosis Society.

Dame Judi Dench made an appearance as Pru Forrest in 1989 for the 10,000th episode. Terry Wogan and Esther Rantzen

were involved with the production of sound for the same episode. Alan Titchmarsh judged Ambridge's entries in the National Gardens Scheme competition in 2003. Radio presenter Chris Moyles appeared in June 2004, Griff Rhys Jones appeared as himself in July 2004 supporting Lynda's campaign to restore the Cat and Fiddle pub. Zandra Rhodes played herself in an episode in September 2006 in connection with a charity fashion show. Mike Gatting appeared as himself in September 2007, in a storyline involving the Village Cup final at Lord's Cricket Ground. Others who have made appearances include Britt Ekland, Humphrey Lyttelton, Anneka Rice, Dame Edna Everage and Antony Gormley.

The Bill

The Bill started on the 16th October 1984 and ended after 27 years on 31st August 2010. Viewers watched the goings-on at Sun Hill Metropolitan Police Station and the surrounding areas of the fictional Borough of Canley, East London. Production and filming had moved several times before settling in Merton, Wimbledon. The programme was created by Geoff McQueen after the successful airing of the drama 'Woodentop' and the series was originally going to be called 'Old Bill'. The long running theme tune 'Overkill' was written by Andy Pask and Charlie Morgan, but it was replaced in 2009. Filming for the series took place all over London including Croydon, Greenwich, Tooting, The London Docklands and particularly the London Borough of Merton.

As with all soaps, The Bill courted controversy at the same time as it received critical acclaim and an army of fans. Due to the subject matter and nature of the show, violent scenes were a part of the format, but this was not well received when episodes were aired before the watershed. In 2008 the show was criticised for featuring a fictional treatment for multiple sclerosis and the MS Society branded the plot 'grossly irresponsible'. Another episode in 2008 culminated in court proceedings, brought by MP George Galloway for defamation of character. He took offence to an episode featuring a corrupt MP who smuggled antiques out of Iraq before the war, which Galloway alleged was a portrayal of him.

At the peak of popularity, The Bill was on air three times a week and the series

THE BILL

was broadcast to more than 55 countries. The Bill was the longest-running police drama series; it took ten years to beat the previous frontrunner Dixon of Dock Green. Each episode concentrated on one shift at Sun Hill and was brought to the audience through the eyes of the characters. The narrative followed the uniformed officers and detectives on their journey to solve crime and uphold law. The programme also explored the troubled personal lives of all the staff at Sun Hill. The Bill was renowned for an excellent cast, supported by some of the country's leading writers and directors who collectively created an admired sense of realism.

The team were extremely particular about production accuracy. The police uniforms used in the series were genuine, again making The Bill unique amongst police dramas. When the series ended, London's Metropolitan Police Service bought most of the police related paraphernalia, including flat caps and stab vests etc. The acquisition was to prevent the costumes falling into the hands of criminals. With attention on authenticity, it caused some irritation that the sirens used in the series were added later in the dubbing suite because The Bill did not have permission to use sirens while on location.

The drama ' Woodentop' featured two lead characters who continued in the same roles in The Bill: Police Constable

Jim Carver (Mark Wingett) and Police Constable June Ackland (Trudie Goodwin). In 2009 the show had a huge cast shake up and many regulars were written out as a result of a fatal fire sweeping through Sun Hill. The new look show wanted to concentrate on more familiar soap opera traits, revealing a more in-depth view of all characters. This revamp presented an opportunity to become more reflective of modern policing with the introduction of officers from ethnic minorities, most notably, Superintendent Adam Okaro. It also allowed coverage of the relationship of homosexual Sergeant Craig Gilmore and PC Luke Ashton.

Other prominent characters included Billy Murray as DS Don Beech, Russell Boulter as DS John Boulton, Tony O'Callaghan as Sergeant Matt Boyden, Peter Ellis as Chief Superintendent Charles Brownlow, Christopher Ellison as DCI Frank Burnside, Eric Richard as Sergeant Bob Cryer, Andrew Paul as PC Dave Quinnan, Lisa Geoghan as PC Polly Page, Jeff Stewart as PC Reg Hollis, Lisa Maxwell as DI Samantha Nixon, Roberta Taylor as Inspector Gina Gold and Graham Cole as PC Tony Stamp.

The Bill broadcast two live episodes, one in 2003 and the second in 2005; Detective Constable Juliet Becker and Constable Cathy Bradford were held hostage by Mark. Cathy raised the custody suite alarm but Juliet was fatally stabbed. The episode was watched by around 11 million viewers. A special programme called 'The Bill Made Me Famous' coincided with the 25th anniversary in which former actors and special guest stars related their time on the show and how it changed their lives including Billy Murray (DS Don Beech), Chris Ellison (DCI Frank Burnside) and popular TV personalities such as Paul O'Grady and Les Dennis.

The last episode of The Bill was filmed in June 2010 and broadcast on the 31st August 2010 followed by a documentary titled 'Farewell The Bill'. Fans of the show started a 'Save the Bill' campaign on Facebook in an effort to convince ITV to re-evaluate the cancellation decision. The story was featured in news bulletins and became a subject for debate. Radio presenter Chris Moyles was one of many to voice an opinion about the closure of Sun Hill. The grand finale featured gang member Jasmine Harris who was involved in the murder of fellow member Liam Martin,

who died in the arms of Inspector Smith after being stabbed. Jasmine was gang raped because she talked to the police. The final episode was specifically written in order to include all cast members; it was watched by 4.4 million viewers.

Over the years guest appearances were made by Keira Knightley, Russell Brand, David Tennant, Paul O'Grady, Sean Bean, Ralf Little, Emma Bunton, Catherine Tate, James McAvoy, Loraine Kelly and Toyah Willcox.

The BBC twice launched a rival series, but 'Merseybeat' lasted for four years and 'HolbyBlue' launched in 2007 only survived one year.

The Bill won several BAFTAs, a Writers' Guild of Great Britain award and the title of 'Best Drama' four times at the Inside Soap Awards. In March 2010, executives at ITV announced that the network did not intend to recommission The Bill, and that filming on the series would cease on the 14th June 2010. The last ever episode of the series was aired on the 31st August 2010.

The Flying Doctors

A series with reference to Australia's Royal Flying Doctors Service aired from 1985 until 1993. The programme was created by Vincent Moran and Terry Stapleton. After an initial six episodes, a further 221 were made boosting the show into worldwide success. The spotlight centred on the lifesaving efforts of the real Royal Flying Doctor Service of Australia. The series was set in the fictional outback town of Cooper's Crossing, a small and isolated rural community.

The cast were comparatively static: Andrew McFarlane was the initial lead role as Dr. Tom Callaghan. Doctor Chris Randall (Liz Burch) joined the crew before McFarlane left during the first season for a break but returned later. Actor Robert Grubb joined the cast as Doctor Geoff Standish. Other profile rich characters included Sister Kate Welling (Lenore Smith), Dr. Guy Reid (David Reyne), pilot Sam Patterson (Peter O'Brien), Rosie 'Rowie' Lang (Sarah Chadwick), mechanic Emma Plimpton (Rebecca Gibney), local policeman Sgt. Jack Carruthers (Terry Gill) and Vic and Nancy Buckley (Maurie Fields and Val Jellay), who ran a small pub, The Majestic, which was also the only boarding facility for many miles.

Storylines were mainly based on the activities of the flying doctors as they raced across the outback. The distances so vast and terrain often too rugged for road vehicles to access the patients, the aircraft and medical staff were the only way expert help could reach those in need. The small posse of doctors and nurses responded to 24-hour call outs from secluded stations and townships across the great Australian

The FLYING DOCTORS

outback. All manner of ailments were treated from snake bites to heat stroke, childbirth to brain surgery and often in near impossible conditions. The series also featured many character driven storylines, a particular favourite being Dr. Standish's romance with Sister Kate Wellings and the amorous interest between Rosie and Johno. After a long awaited proposal acceptance, Rosie and Johno arranged a wedding ceremony to take place on the RFDS air strip. At the last minute Rosie gets cold feet and the guests are left waiting along with the groom.

The popular series ran for nine seasons and was successfully screened internationally to over 50 countries. Rating figures began to dip towards the end of the eighth series and producers decided a revamp was necessary. The setting was changed to Broken Hill and the title changed to RFDS. The new format did not revive viewership and the show lasted just one season.

The Grove Family

The Grove Family is now recognised as the first soap opera on British television. The first episode of The Grove Family aired on 8th April 1954 and was written by father-and-son team Ronald and Michael Pertwee. All episodes were broadcast live from the BBC's Lime Grove Studios, which provided the inspiration for the title of the series.

The series followed the story of a run-of-the-mill British family, living regular lives in a domestic setting in Hendon, north London. The family was designed to reflect the average post-war family. The house was quite full with father of the house Bob (Edward Evans), his wife Grace (Ruth Dunning), Grace's mother, known to all as 'Gran' (Nancy Roberts) and four children Jack, Pat, Daphne and Lennie. Bob worked as a builder and was the principal wage earner in the house. Grace Grove was in charge in the kitchen and responsible for the family's wellbeing. Gran was a comical burden with her endless requests for a cup of tea and being 'faint from lack of nourishment'. The weekly events of the family were free of tragedy and the histrionics that have become the norm in soaps today. The show was fond of weaving useful information and current topics into the storylines. References were made to current affairs, the education act and an episode featured a policeman showing Bob Grove how to safeguard his home from burglars.

A prominent fan was the Queen Mother, who remarked that the family was "so English, so real!" The series came to an end on the 28th June 1957 with the most dramatic incident in the show's

three-year history. The family holiday ended with a theatrical air-sea rescue. Very few episodes survive in the archives; only three of the original 148 episodes.

In 1995 The Grove Family was featured in a film titled 'It's a Great Day'. Filming moved away from the Lime Grove studios and scenes were shot at Shepperton Studios instead.

In 1991, to mark the anniversary of Lime Grove Studios, the BBC recreated one of the early episodes of The Grove Family. Sue Johnston played Grace, Leslie Grantham was Bob, Anna Wing portrayed Gran and Nick Berry played Jack.

The Newcomers

A 1960s English soap opera The Newcomers was broadcast twice a week in thirty-minute episodes. The show began on the 5th October 1965 and was on air until the 28th November 1969. It was created by Colin Morris and initially produced by Verity Lamb. The Newcomers was the BBC's most successful continuing drama serial before EastEnders and the theme music was composed by John Barry.

The focus of the show was centred on the Cooper family. The Coopers moved from London to a rural housing estate in fictional Angleton. Ellis (Alan Browning) and Vivienne Cooper (Maggie Fitzgibbon) decided to move when Ellis's employer opened a new factory in the rural village. Ellis worked for a light industrial manufacturing company called Eden Brothers. The Newcomers explored the impact of the innovative factory on locals and the new arrivals. Social issues were examined and the contrasting lives of the factory workers, the management and the local community. Common themes followed the interaction of mixing working class with middle and upper class, the evolving story of love affairs between the social hierarchy and the power struggle of factory management. Storylines switched between work and home.

The Coopers were not the only characters to struggle with the move. Many of the relocated workers also had trouble living outside the city. As the series developed, problems on the factory floor trickle into community life. Throughout the constant struggle, the Coopers endeavoured to raise their children to a high standard but the youngsters had plenty

of their own difficulties to contend with.

The most prominent character was Vivienne Cooper who gained enormous popularity with the viewers; the press referred to her as 'the BBC's answer to Elsie Tanner'.

The cast included several actors who later achieved wider fame, including Jenny Agutter, Wendy Richard, Alan Browning and Judy Geeson.

The Newcomers popularity never waned during the four-year run. The show began to suffer behind the scenes after Ellis was the victim of a fatal heart attack and actor Alan Browning left the show.

The Sullivans

The Sullivans was an Australian television series produced by Crawford Productions and broadcast on Nine Network. It started on the 15th November 1976 and ended on the 10th March 1983. The story revolved around a family living in Melbourne and the effect World War II had on their lives and was set in1939 as war was declared on Germany. It remained a constant ratings success in Australia and was also popular in the UK, Ireland, Netherlands, Gibraltar and New Zealand. The series was sold to over 45 countries worldwide and ran for a total of 11 series and 1,114 episodes. Fourteen writers worked on the initial episodes and it is reputed to have cost one million dollars to set up production; a mammoth budget for 1976. The series was celebrated for its high standards and historical accuracy. Scenes were often time stamped and referenced genuine military deployments. Researchers faithfully recreated sets and sourced replica or actual food packaging from 1939.

The Sullivan family lived at 7 Gordon Street in Victoria; the family unit consisted of the parents and their four children. The show was popular for the realistic portrayal of the Sullivan family and their neighbours during the Second World War. Plots were character driven and rarely relied on melodramatics.

Key characters were Grace Sullivan (Lorraine Bayly) the matriarch and killed during an air raid in London where she had gone to be reunited with her eldest son John. Grace was married to Dave Sullivan (Paul Cronin), a hard-working patriarch and World War I veteran. Dave was killed in a car accident in 1948. John,

the Sullivans

a medical student was the eldest son, missing in action for two years before he was found convalescing in England. Tom (Steven Tandy) was the second son who was in active service for the majority of the series and later married Patty Spencer (Penny Downie). Terry (Richard Morgan) was the third son and was a prisoner of war in Changi Prison. He was psychologically injured from his war experience and became a troubled man; he was jailed in 1946 for armed robbery, escaped and became a fugitive. Kitty (Susan Hannaford) was the youngest child who became a nurse. Other popular characters included Uncle Harry (Michael Caton) and his wife Rose (Maggie Dence), Maggie Hayward (Vikki Hammond) a divorcee and landlady of the local pub. Ida

Jessup (Vivean Gray) was the Sullivans' English-born neighbour from Battersea. Hans, Lottie and daughter Anna (Ingrid Mason) were German immigrants who owned the local shop. Hans and Lottie were interned as enemy aliens but Anna escaped by hastily marrying John Sullivan.

Numerous actors were cast in short-term roles, this enabled young actors to gain early experience before going on to experience enormous success and the likes of Mel Gibson, Kerry Armstrong, Kylie Minogue, Dannii Minogue, Sam Neill, Gary Sweet and Sigrid Thornton were among them.

The Sullivans attracted critical acclaim and it was one of Australia's most popular drama series, but British Show 'Are You Being Served?' was ahead of The Sullivans in the soap ratings table. The Sullivans was awarded five Logies in 1978: Paul Cronin won 'Most Popular Australian Actor', Lorraine Bayly won 'Most Popular Australian Actress, Michael Caton won 'Best Sustained Performance by an Actor in a Supporting Role', Vivean Gray won 'Best Sustained Performance by an Actress in a Supporting Role' and the show won Most Popular Australian Drama.

The Waltons

The Waltons was an American television, series created by Earl Hamner Jr and the basis of his book, 'Spencer's Mountain'. The series began on the 14th September 1972 and it played for nine seasons. Earl Hamner also narrated each episode as the voice of John-Boy Walton. Earl Hamner's film 'The Homecoming' was the pilot movie for The Waltons. It was not initially planned as a pilot for a series but it was popular enough for a series to be commissioned.

The show took place during the Depression and subsequently during World War II. Reflecting family life in a rural Virginia community, the story unfolded around Walton's Mountain, a fictional town in Jefferson County. The town of Walton's Mountain was built behind the Warner Bros Studios.

Earl Hamner drew on his many life experiences to assist in the creation of the characters, storylines and the wholesome, Walton family values.

John and Olivia had eight children of which there were three girls and five boys. John-Boy, Jason, Mary-Ellen, Erin, Ben, twins Jim-Bob and Joseph, and Elizabeth. Joseph died at birth. John's parents also lived with them; Esther and Zeb. Patricia Neal and Andrew Duggan starred as Olivia and John Walton, with Edgar Bergen and Ellen Corby as Grandpa and Grandma Walton, Richard Thomas as oldest son John-Boy Walton, Judy Norton-Taylor (Mary-Ellen), Mary Beth McDonough (Erin), Kami Cotler (Elizabeth), Eric Scott (Ben), David W. Harper (Jim-Bob) and Jon Walmsley (Jason).

Other regular characters included

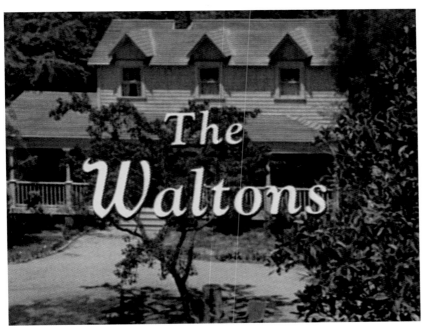

the Baldwin sisters, two aged spinsters who distilled moonshine, known as 'Papa's recipe', Ike Godsey as postmaster and owner of the general store with his high and mighty wife Corabeth. There was also Verdie and Harley Foster, Maude, Flossie Brimmer and gossip Yancy Tucker. The series finale, 'The Revel', revolved around a party and the invitation date was given as June 4th 1946. A span of 13 years is covered in 9 seasons. During the 1970s, viewers saw real life events reflected in the show with Grandma Esther Walton suffering a stroke and the death of her on-screen husband, Grandpa Zeb Walton, played by Will Geer, who died in 1978.

The characters and viewers were

immersed in history as the time line followed the American Civil Wars, The Hindenburg disaster, the abdication of King Edward VIII, the death of President Roosevelt, the invasion of Pearl Harbour, World War II, the assassination of President J. F. Kennedy and the moon landing. World War II deeply affected the family and all four Walton boys enlisted in the military; John-Boy's plane was shot down. Six feature-length movies were made and three reunion movies were produced in the 1990s for CBS: 'A Walton Thanksgiving Reunion' in 1993, 'A Walton Wedding' in 1995 and 'A Walton Easter' in 1997. All featured the original cast with the exception of the late Will Geer.

The Waltons' first season brought critical acclaim and several awards. Both Richard Thomas and Michael Learned took home Best Actor Emmys, Ellen Corby was awarded the Best Supporting Actress honour and the series was given the Emmy for Outstanding Drama Series. The show also earned Emmys for writing and editing in addition to receiving the prestigious Peabody award. The show won 19 Emmy awards in total. The final episode aired in June 1981 was called 'Good night John Boy'.

The Young Doctors

The Young Doctors was an Australian soap opera, first screened on the 8th November 1976 on the Nine Network. Eight series were broadcast and a total of 1,396 episodes, ending on the 30th March 1983. The series was created and produced by Reg Grundy Organisation, and later by Sue Masters.

The show had a long run considering the ridiculed production had a notoriously bad set and little variance in storylines other than weddings. The hospital-based drama focused on the staff at the Albert Memorial Hospital. Plots involving romance were the norm and very little attention was given to any medical procedures or issues. Bunnys was a club setting that allowed more saturation of storylines relating to the personal life and romances of the staff.

The first series was launched at the same time as The Sullivans, but with an incredibly low budget in comparison to the acclaimed Sullivans series. Cast were encouraged to wear their own clothes in a bid to reduce the costs of the costume department. The result of a poor production budget was very evident on screen in the early years and the soap featured no location filming at all.

Iconic characters were Sister Grace Scott (Cornelia Frances) who portrayed the strict and officious Sister and was the show's villain. A far more popular character was kiosk lady Ada Simmonds (Gwen Plumb). Dr Graham Steele (Tim Page) played the apathetic medic. Alfred Sandor was known as the rather aristocratic head surgeon. Chris King portrayed the friendly orderly Dennis Jameson, Michael Beecher a suave superintendent. Dr Brian Denham was

CELEBRATING 50 YEARS of AUSSIE TV

attended by his loyal secretary Helen Gordon.

The Young Doctors was due to be axed soon after the 13-pilot episodes had aired, however it was reprieved and continued running. Fans blame the advent of one-day cricket as being responsible for altering the show's schedule and a resulting decline in ratings that led to the series cancellation in 1982.

Soap Quiz: Questions

1. What was the first Australian soap to be shown on British TV?

2. Which future pop star played Beth Brennan in Neighbours?

3. Which was the first British soap to feature a test-tube baby?

4. Which character was found dead in the first episode of Eastenders?

5. In Coronation Street, who rescued Bet Lynch when the Rover's Return caught fire?

6. Which family moved into 13, Coronation Street in 1964?

7. Who played Lofty in Eastenders?

8. Which British soap was set in Glendarrock?

9. Which Coronation Street character was killed on Blackpool sea front in 1989?

10. In Eastenders which character won £10,000 at bingo?

11. Who played Meg Mortimer in Crossroads?

12. What three surnames did the character played by Joan Collins in Dynasty have?

13. In Eastenders who spent four months in jail after a road accident on Christmas Eve 1992?

CORONATION STREET

14. Who opened the Old School Tearooms in Emmerdale with money from her divorce settlement?

15. Who did Gail Lewis marry in Neighbours?

16. What was the name of the restaurant run by the Di Marco family in Eastenders?

17. Who did Emily Bishop take in as a lodger in November 1983?

18. What was the name of the baby that Pam and Bobby Ewing adopted in Dallas?

19. What was Lofty's real name in Eastenders?

20. In which 1960s British soap did Jenny Agutter play Kirsty Kerr?

21. Who was the creator of "Coronation Street"?

22. What was the series originally to be called?

23. What was Valerie Barlow's maiden name?

24. What were the names of Deirdre's THREE husbands?

25. Who were the landlords of The Rover's Return when the series started?

26. Which soap opera is set in the fictional county of Borsetshire?

27. As at 2004, which actor is the only member of the original "Coronation Street" cast who is still in the show?

28. What is the name of the fictional tube station in "Eastenders"?

29. In "Brookside", which character murdered her father and buried him under the patio and was also involved in the first lesbian kiss in a UK soap opera?

30. In which of the following soap operas has Oscar winning actor Russell Crowe appeared? "Neighbours", "Home And Away" or "The Flying Doctors"?

31. First shown on the station's launch night, what is Channel 5's first original soap opera called?

32. Originally starting as a six part series in 1957, "Calling Nurse Roberts", what was Britain's first medical soap and also the first serial to be shown twice-weekly?

33. In which year did "Emmerdale Farm" become "Emmerdale"? 1989, 1992 or 1995?

34. At the first British Soap Awards in 1999, which "Eastenders" actress won the "sexiest female" award?

35. How many episodes of "Prisoner: Cell Block H" were made?

36. In which fictional town do the residents of Coronation Street live?

37. In what year was Coronation Street first broadcast?

38. What is the name of the pub in Coronation Street?

39. What animal did Jack Duckworth keep?

40. In what year was EastEnders first broadcast?

41. Who is the longest serving character?

42. What was the name of Ethel's Dog?

43. In which county is Emmerdale set?

44. What was dropped from the name of the show in 1989?

45. In December 1993 what killed four of the Villagers?

46. Zac, Lisa, Marlon, Belle & Cain share what surname?

47. Hollyoaks is set in which City?

48. What is the name of the pub in Hollyoaks?

49. Which soap broadcast the first Pre-watershed Lesbian Kiss in 1994?

50. Which family who lived at No 5 were the first family to move in?

Soap Quiz: Answers

1. The Sullivans

2. Natalie Imbruglia

3. Crossroads

4. Reg Cox

5. Kevin Webster

6. The Ogdens

7. Tom Watt

8. Take the High Road

9. Alan Bradley

10. Dot Cotton

11. Noelle Gordon

12. Carrington, Colby and Dexter

13. Pat Butcher

14. Kathy Tate

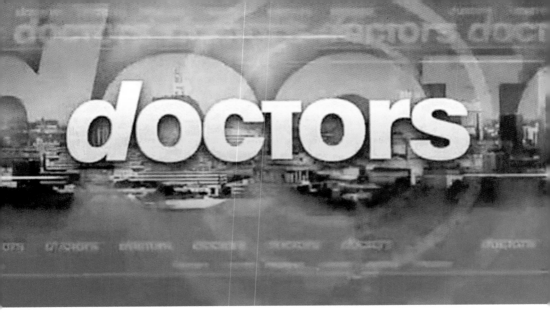

25. Jack and Annie Walker

26. The Archers

27. William Roache

28. Walford East

29. Beth Jordache

30. Neighbours

31. Family Affairs

32. Emergency – Ward 10

33. 1989

34. Tamzin Outhwaite

35. 692

36. Weatherfield

37. 1960

38. Rover's Return

39. Pigeon

40. 1985

41. Ian Beale

42. Willy

43. Yorkshire

44. Farm

**The pictures in this book were provided
courtesy of the following:**

WIKICOMMONS
commons.wikimedia.org

Design & Artwork by Scott Giarnese

Published by Demand Media Limited

Publishers: Jason Fenwick & Jules Gammond

Written by Thea Tsamplakos